AWAKENING

UFOS AND OTHER STRANGE HAPPENINGS

PETER MAXWELL SLATTERY

With a foreword by Jason Gleaves

AWAKENING: UFOs and Other Strange Happenings

© 2020 by Peter Maxwell Slattery

Cover by Kesara (Christine Dennett), www.kesara.org

Editor: Jessica Bryan, www.oregoneditor.com

DISCLAIMER: The information in this book is intended to be of a general educational nature, and does not constitute medical, legal, or other professional advice for any specific individual or situation.

No part of this book may be reproduced or transmitted in any form or by any means, without permission in writing from the publisher.

Published by Peter Maxwell Slattery

Email: petermaxwellslattery@outlook.com.au

Website: www.petermaxwellslattery.com

ISBN: 978-0-244-26223-5

DEDICATION

This book is dedicated to all Beings throughout all planes and in-between, throughout the universe and beyond.

THANK YOU!

A big thank you goes out to my family, friends, and all my supporters and fellow Beings from the many realms in this universe and beyond for their love and support, and I also thank Shi-Ji.

Love, light, and bliss,

Peter Maxwell Slattery

TESTIMONIALS

What experts are saying about Peter Maxwell Slattery, his evidence, and his experiences.

"In the top 1% of authentic experiencer cases in Ufology to-date".

Jason Gleaves - (Ex-Royal Air Force and British Aerospace) Image Analysis Expert

"Our remote viewing projects have determined the legitimacy of what he continually experiences".

John Vivanco - Remote Viewer

CONTENTS

Foreword - *By Jason Gleaves*……………………………12

Preface……………………………………………………………14

Introduction……………………………………………………16

PART ONE: PARANORMAL INVESTIGATIONS: 17

Chapter 1: First Sighting……………………………….18

Chapter 2: UFOs and Ghosts……………………..…….25

Chapter 3: Beechworth Ghost Girls…………………33

Chapter 4: UFOs Over Lavy……………………………38

Chapter 5: Ghost Hunting……………………………….47

Chapter 6: Remote Viewing, UFOs, and Psychic Aliens……………………………………………………………60

Chapter 7: The Monte Cristo Homestead………..70

Chapter 8: Remote Viewing, Meditation, and The Blue Guy……………………………………………………….77

Chapter 9: Ghost Hunting and the Hume Highway UFO..82

Chapter 10: Daytime Sightings and The Red Orb..98

Chapter 11: Red Light Hill...................................108

Chapter 12: The Blue Orb...................................114

Chapter 13: Visited By a Light Being..................119

Chapter 14: Beam Ship.......................................122

PART TWO: MEETING SHI-JI: 128

Chapter 15: The Visitor......................................129

Chapter 16: After Effect.....................................136

Chapter 17: Psychic Predictions........................144

Chapter 18: Orb With A Face............................148

Chapter 19: Black Helicopters..........................153

Chapter 20: Shi-Ji Flies By................................156

Chapter 21: Life Seems Mundane....................159

Chapter 22: The Light Being Pops In Again……..163

Chapter 23: Shi-Ji Drops In……………………………..166

Chapter 24: Visions……………………………………….176

Chapter 25: Shi-Ji Comes Calling…………………..180

Chapter 26: Thinking About the Past……………189

Chapter 27: Shi-Ji Tells All……………………………..193

Chapter 28: Goodbye and Hello……………………208

Chapter 29: Flickers of Light in the House……..214

Chapter 30: Confirmation……………………………..218

Chapter 31: Bluey………………………………………….224

Chapter 32: Unexpected Message…………………228

Chapter 33: Revelations and Where to Go From Here…………………………………………………………….231

Books by Peter Maxwell Slattery…………………..235

About the Author…………………………………………236

FOREWORD

By Jason Gleaves

When Peter contacts me with images or footage to be analyzed, I know something special is going to manifest. Whether it's unexplained aerial objects or Extra-Terrestrial beings, nothing surprises me anymore.

My job is so enjoyable and heart-warming when I get to see firsthand and analyze this kind of UFO phenomena coming from people in every walk of life, worldwide.

I have known Peter for a few years now, and our paths crossed not by mistake but through my own thirst for knowledge regarding the deep rabbit hole of ufology.

Peter's dedication and personal drive in ufology are commendable and hugely inspirational to others wanting to follow this tricky, uneven path, if only to enlighten their minds or to just simply answer those niggling questions about who, why and, what is this all about.

I have stated in the past that I class Peter's material of video footage and imagery to be in the top one percent of authenticity in ufology, worldwide, and I stand by this to this day.

His work goes to show that we are being visited here on Earth by multiple off-world races and beings that are inter-dimensional in nature.

The images in this book that Peter has asked me to analyze in more detail, using the most up-to-date software available, have revealed surprising results. They have all gone through the same process of (image) upscaling to reduce the visual pixilation of the original source images during the analyzing process. In addition, enlargement and enhancements such as filters have been used, which help immensely in revealing hidden detail not always seen in its original raw format.

Jason Gleaves, Ufonly and International Author of UFO PHOTO and The Ufology Umbrella, Ex-Royal Air Force and British Aerospace, Airbus.

PREFACE

After a lifetime of experiences, it's amazing I didn't connect the dots until sooner. The first lot started at the age of seven, when I had a female voice in my head telling me things before they happened. My parents even took me to the doctors over this, and the doctor just said, "Well...the voice is not telling him anything bad." That's all he had to say. Later I found out who was behind these telepathic / thought transfer communications.

With that said, many times between the ages of eight and twelve, I had many experiences of waking up to what is commonly referred to as the classic "grey alien" in my room, except it was white. I found out later who this being was and its purpose for visiting me. I never equated it to an alien visitation, aliens, angels, or demons. These things didn't come to mind.

Not until many years later, and even now, I am still unraveling what's going on, and I ask myself, *Why me, and why are millions of people on the planet having paranormal experiences?*

It all comes down to humanity going through a dark storm before the light can shine again. This light is actually in each and every one of us, but to come to this conclusion, well...let's just say, you will have to follow me on my journey to understand what I've discovered, why and how.

What you are about to read was written at the time the events described were unfolding. From this and my other books you will learn how my understanding of the paranormal grew deeper, and how my life was changed by my unusual experiences. I was very innocent and ignorant of many things in the beginning. But over time, from experience and interactions, information came to me quickly and grew exponentially. Universal understanding came to light in an unimaginable proportion.

Welcome to my story.

Peter Maxwell Slattery

INTRODUCTION

Awakening – UFOs and Other Strange Happenings is an account of the unusual experiences I've had since I was twelve years old.

Part One documents the timeline of these experiences, including witnessing apparitions and seeing alien spacecrafts, also known as "UFOs." Ghost hunting and remote viewing are also covered.

Part Two describes how I "met" Shi-Ji, a Being from the Pleiades, and the teachings I received from her, especially teachings about "The Shift."

Come and join me on the life-changing ride into the unknown that has shaped and molded the person I am today.

Please note that names have been altered to protect the identities of some of the people mentioned in this book.

So...sit back, relax, and have an open mind.

Peace, love, light, and bliss to all.

Peter Maxwell Slattery

PART ONE

PARANORMAL INVESTIGATIONS

CHAPTER 1

FIRST SIGHTING

It's an "out of this world" experience to see a UFO.

My first sighting was in the summer of 1995 in the suburb of Lavington, which is in the City of Albury in the state of New South Wales, Australia. It was a hot, sunny day when I walked north on Dick Road to the Petrol Station to get a Slurpee.

While taking in my surroundings, looking northeast I noticed a huge grey disc in the sky, just right of Red Light Hill, which is a huge hill north of Lavington. The object was at least the size of three football fields. It was just hovering and then it started to move west. I just stood there dumbfounded.

I looked at the object for about 30 or 40 seconds as it hovered west towards the hill; then it passed the hill and continued west until it went out of view.

In trying to come to grips with what I had just seen, my first thought was: *I've got to tell somebody.* But I didn't. I was a strange kid and I didn't think anyone would believe me.

Given the number of sightings and paranormal experiences I have had since this early one, I now know what I'm looking at. The average person, when hearing about a UFO, usually just blows it off. Now…I don't want people to blindly believe me. I've had a hard enough time trying to comprehend what's been happening to me. I just want people to be skeptical and come to their own conclusions, but please keep an open mind.

It is now estimated that between 200 and 400 billion planets exist in our galaxy alone. Slowly, the concept that humanity is not the only intelligent civilization in the universe is becoming more and more acceptable to the average person.

From writings in the scriptures about "supernatural beings," to all religions having a connection to the stars, the alien reality is real. To date, over 500 military witnesses have come forward about their knowledge of Extra-

Terrestrial (E.T.) reality. More and more disclosure groups and UFO organizations are popping up worldwide.

From presidents, to military personnel, to police officers, to the average person, all types of people have and are witnessing UFOs. In recent times the alien abduction phenomenon has increased and, so too, have UFO sightings worldwide.

Some people say the alien abduction scenario is sleep paralysis and the people having these experiences are delusional. But this doesn't account for well-documented cases such as Betty and Barney Hill, Travis Walton, and many others, because they were awake during their experiences.

Also, physical evidence has been obtained in many cases, including witness testimonies, videos, and photographs. How could people worldwide describe the same types of experiences when encountering aliens and UFOs if these events are a hoax?

It's the same with crop circles. Most of them are not even circles, but geometric patterns and pictures, and they are popping up overnight, worldwide. If humans created these overnight crop circles, they would have needed aerial assistance and a lot of manpower, which would be impossible to cover up.

This would be impossibly complicated for people to do in a short amount of time. Also, plants are being affected in terms of their makeup and structure, which is altered during these events. Simply stated, there is a ton of evidence out there that the E.T reality exists. Though, on the odd occasion there are hoaxes.

Now…back my story… I have documented most of my experiences with the date and time of the events, which do not just happen around the place where I live. They seem to happen in other places, too. The paranormal can manifest anywhere and anytime.

Documenting these types of incidents tends to be a trend in the UFO field, because sometimes you get corresponding evidence—on the odd occasion when somebody else reports the same event. This adds validity to the claim.

While coming to terms at the start of my frequent experiences with UFOs, and convincing myself that I was not insane, I was led to investigate everything paranormal, because UFOs aren't the only unusual things to be discovered.

I have witnessed apparitions, or "ghosts," as they are commonly called, not just once or twice, but many times—as you will read in the following paragraphs.

Also included is a description of seeing orbs (balls of light). I experience this all the time. And other people see them around me more often than I do. Trippy stuff like this is always happening.

In starting to investigate all things paranormal, I created "Investigators For The Truth" ("IFTT"), which was a paranormal society with two investigators, and "UFO UPDATE DAILY AUSTRALIA," in which I helped to validate, debunk, and/or teach people about the paranormal, and how these events are actually normal.

Doing this helped me learn more about the E.T reality from others, because I was documenting UFO sightings and reports from around Australia and the entire world. During this time, I conducted investigations for free, because some people have no one to turn to for help. I also investigated well-known haunted locations.

Some of the investigations in this book were done as a result of being asked by a homeowner to find out if their place was haunted, or because I have received repeated emails on a reported location having activity. Some investigations are conducted just for fun, such as "Monte Cristo," Australia's most famous haunted house.

This book was written to help people who have gone through, or who are currently having experiences similar to mine. My purpose is to help others who have no one to turn to, and let each person know they are not alone.

Sharing my story is a good outlet for releasing my feelings and sharing my knowledge, and when put together with other legitimate alien contact and abductee stories, it makes for one of the most important true stories ever—the point of which is: "We are not alone."

There is no way I can keep my story to myself, because paranormal experiences have affected every aspect of my life. I have also discovered that writing, talking, and educating people about how the paranormal is actually normal is part of my reason for being here.

Over the years, I have received hundreds of videos of UFOs, occurring in Australia. From the rest of the world, I have received thousands of videos. So it seems these experiences have become common among humans. How could this be captured on photos and videos if it is not real?

You will learn in this book about the conditions under which my experiences occurred, the dates, and a few specific times. Also included is photographic evidence, actual pictures taken on both photo and video cameras during the daytime and at night.

CHAPTER 2

UFOs AND GHOSTS

After the time of my first sighting, nothing else happened for a while. Just like my friends, I finished tenth grade, left school, and went out into the world. I left home and moved to Wollongong, and eventually moved back to Albury and got my own place.

At this time in my life, I had started a rap career and a new job as a cleaner to keep the money coming in. I didn't think much about UFOs during that time, but I was interested in them because of the sighting when I was younger.

In 2004, I had my next sighting, and this time a friend saw it, too. It was summer again, a hot day after work, and my friend David and I were on our way to my place in the afternoon.

On the way home, just around the corner from my place on Eden Street, there was this huge ball of white / orange light hovering in the air over the suburb of Glenroy. I immediately pulled over to the side of the road and we hopped out.

The object was going up, down, and across, and making other unconventional maneuvers. It was just flying all over the place.

The light coming from it was like the light from a star. It was so bright!

David and I watched this for two or three minutes, during which time a couple of cars also pulled up and others watched the object. Then all of a sudden it vanished.

When we arrived home a minute later, a few friends were at my house with my brother. I told everyone what happened and they just blew it off, except from my brother. But I couldn't shut up about it for the rest of the night.

David looked like his whole world had been turned upside down, although he eventually got over it. But I couldn't "get over it," because I knew it was an "out of this world" experience.

A few months after this second UFO sighting, I started working at the TAFE institute in Albury as a cleaner. This is when I had one of my first paranormal experience with ghosts, and it didn't just happen once.

After asking if I wanted the job, my new boss asked me if I believed in ghosts. I told him I was open-minded. Then he told me the Kitchen Block was haunted.

During this conversation, he basically warned me to watch out, because encountering one of these "ghosts" was a possibility. I took him seriously, and soon enough, it happened. And it continued to happen on a number of occasions during the time I worked at TAFE.

What I witnessed was crazy. It changed my world and scared the absolute crap out of me. If only I could have filmed my reaction.

The first week at TAFE, I saw shadows moving around out of the corner of my eye and didn't think much about it.

After taking notice and keeping track of when it was happening, a couple of times I saw what people now call "Shadow People." These are ghosts that look like shadows in human form. At first, I would notice one and then it would dart off. These shadow people are so fast it's unbelievable.

After this had been happening for about a month, it started to get even more intense. It's really hard to explain. I would be cleaning in the kitchens and this thing would come right up to me, realize that I had seen it, and then float quickly past me.

In the same building, there was another room where the toilets were on the ground floor, towards the back of the block. In this room, you could hear coughing and loud bangs for no reason at all. The funny thing is that I was just a floor cleaner and maintained the outside of the buildings. Someone else was responsible for the toilets.

Now...the person who cleaned the toilets witnessed similar things at random times, and some of this happened when we were around each other. So it was good that someone else witnessed it, too. He had worked there before me, and he told me about some of his past experiences, which were identical to what I was witnessing. I got a feeling of dread in the toilet area and only went there once.

Another strange thing is that occasionally I witnessed the shadow man running down the stairs, and then he would just disappear. After investigating, I found out the place on the stairs where I had seen the shadow man was the actual location where a man had died from slipping on the stairs. Also I found out that the toilet area, where I heard noises and coughing, is where a person died from an asthma attack.

Now…there were two sets of stairs and a few different toilet rooms. So I didn't know exactly if this was linked to the deaths in the area where these events occurred. But when the sightings and experiences matched up with the scenes of the actual deaths (according to my boss), it sent chills down my back, because I hadn't known how and where these people died when I accepted the job.

So in other words, I didn't know where they died until months later when I asked the boss. When I did, the locations where the paranormal activity occurred precisely matched where people had died a traumatic death.

Well...that was trippy!

Later I found out through my research that these experiences at the TAFE were mainly "residual hauntings." It's known in the paranormal community that there are two types of hauntings. The first is a residual haunting, which is when the ghost doesn't know you are there. It just does the same things over and over, like a tape player on repeat.

The second is an "intelligent haunting." This is when the ghost can interact with you, move objects around, and so forth.

Another aspect is that some ghosts have never been in human form. Some of these beings are known as "elementals" (nature spirits), and some are "otherworldly beings."

After my time at TAFE, I moved to Melbourne for four years to pursue my rap career after recording my first album: *I'VE ONLY JUST B-GUN*. I thought: *I'm young, so why not*. In Melbourne, I worked as a cleaner and recorded another five albums. Leaving Melbourne, I went to the Gold Coast for a short time and then moved back to Albury to be around family and friends and start reorganizing my life.

By the time I finished my rap career—after recording another six albums in 2009—my outlook on life had changed. In early 2010, I started the paranormal society "IFTT" and "UFO UPDATE DAILY AUSTRALIA," because the idea of paranormal activity had never left my mind and I had a lot of questions. I started to investigate and research anything and everything that had to do with the paranormal.

Soon enough, I was getting publicity for IFTT and had started to do a few investigations here and there. Although I investigated many places, things didn't really get going until late 2010—not just in the paranormal ghost hunting field, but also in the UFO field.

At this time, I started a new job at an accounting firm in Albury doing a "Business Certificate 3 Traineeship." Life was good because I had security and structure. But soon all that would change, because I started having more paranormal experiences, which led to it becoming an obsession. I was looking everywhere for answers.

CHAPTER 3

BEECHWORTH GHOST GIRLS

On the 27th of June 2010, I planned to drive to Beechworth, about 40 minutes out of Albury, over the border in the state of Victoria. I planned to do a pre-investigation at the Beechworth Jail gardens. There were reports of paranormal activity at Beechworth, so I thought I would check into it.

By pre-investigation I mean visiting a reported haunted location by myself during the day, so when I go there at night, I know where the hazards are. Ghost hunting takes place in the dark with an infrared camera mainly. I use this type of camera to see in the dark.

Also I do E.M.F (electromagnetic field) meter readings, which pick up abnormal readings. This can mean there is paranormal activity in the area—it's theorized that spirits use and manipulate the electromagnetic field in order to manifest. Sometimes a high reading can be due to poor electrical wiring which can make people feel like there is a presence, among other things as well.

I arrived at Beechworth at around 10:30 in the morning. It was a beautiful day for ghost hunting. I scanned the gardens for hazards, did an E.M.F sweep, took a few pictures and notes, and that was that.

Later, when I got back home, I decided to flick through the pictures on the computer, just for something to do. Guess what I came across? A few ghosts in one of my photos! When I zoomed in on the viewfinder, I realized it looked like a woman holding a baby, with a young girl in front of her.

During the coming days, I insisted everyone look at it. No one knew what to think. I could see it clearly, and so could many other people, without me even pointing it out.

In the weeks after, I looked for any information I could find on the people who once lived in the house at the Beechworth Jail. All I could find out was the connecting house to the Jail was used by the Governor of the town at one time, and the

Superintendent of the police force at another time.

So were these apparitions from the Governors' or the Superintendents' families? Who knows? The possibilities are endless.

I gave them a name: "The Beechworth Ghost Girls."

All I know is they were there and the camera captured their images, but I didn't see them at the time. This really made me think about dimensions and how we really can't see everything that is happening here and in the universe around us.

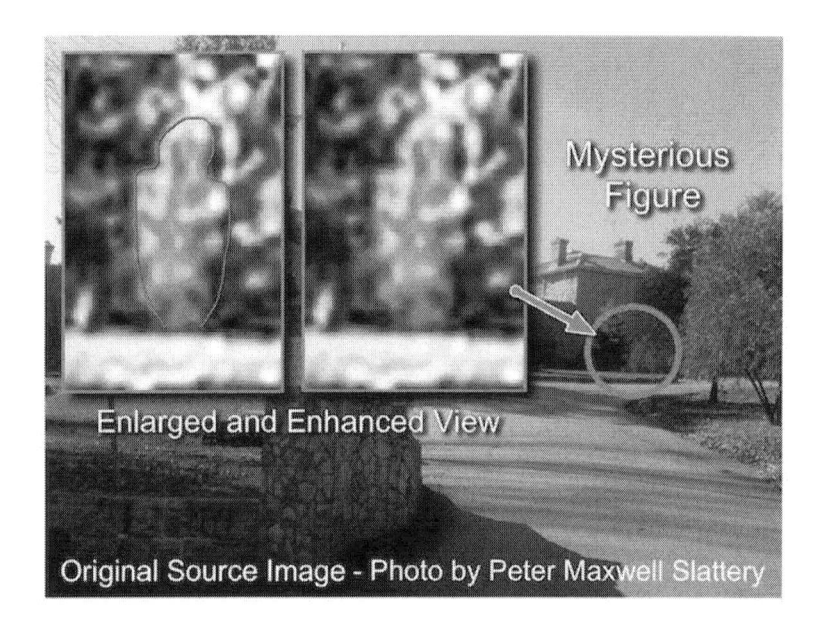

Photo of "The Beechworth Ghost Girls" – In this image analyzed by Jason Gleaves, he has outlined the predominate figure which appears to be that of a little girl in the top left box. In the circle you can see the apparitions from the original photo.

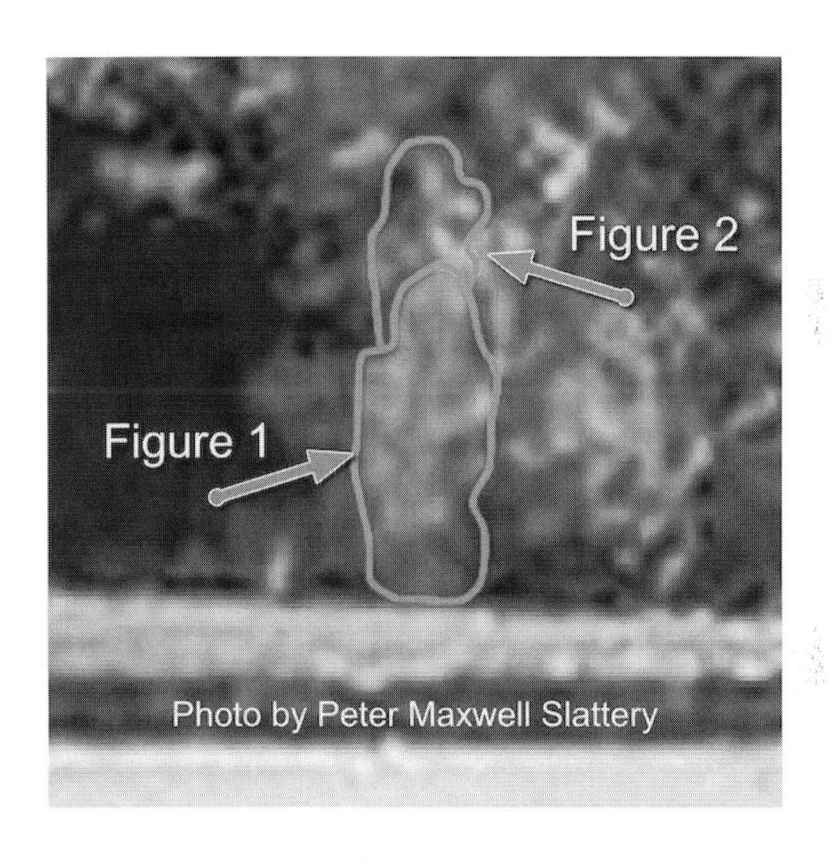

Close-up image that has been analyzed by Jason Gleaves. Figure 1: Small girl. Figure 2: What appears to be a lady holding a baby.

CHAPTER 4

UFOS OVER LAVY

Soon the strange occurrences would start getting closer to home.

It was the 10th of October 2010 and a good friend of mine named William was over at my place in the suburb of Lavington (also known as Lavy) in Albury.

William was out in front, about to leave, when he called me by my nickname, "Poyda, come and see this."

When I walked to the front door and looked at where he was pointing, I saw an object that resembled exactly what I had seen six years earlier. It was doing the same maneuvers flying near Nail Can Hill.

Immediately, I grabbed the video camera and started filming.

While we watched, William debated what it was. It wasn't a helicopter, and it wasn't a plane, because a plane would drop out of the sky if it was moving that slow, and going backwards and forwards, down and up.

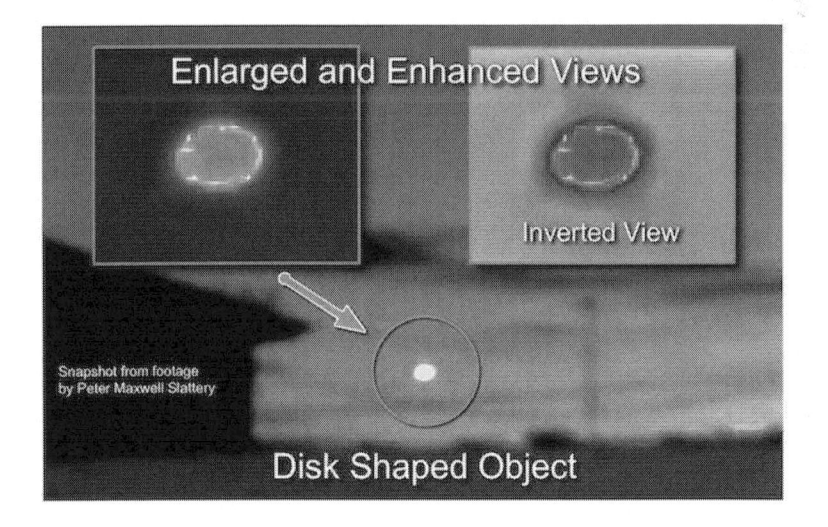

Close-up snapshot of the UFO from the 10th of October 2010 video analyzed by Jason Gleaves.

William couldn't work out what it was, but I knew. I filmed a bit over a minute's worth of footage on video in which you can see him, the object, and the conditions under which we observed it.

Afterwards I put it in the back of my mind, but it was hard, because this happened another five times in the next month. William was there for three of the sightings. He saw it twice at my house and once at his place around the corner from my house.

On the 17th of October 2010, late at night, I had another experience that proved to me that these UFOs were "not of this world." I had just bought a telescope and while outside testing it and taking photos through it, I had another sighting.

I was familiar with the night sky, and after being outside for well over half an hour I saw something very odd and knew it was not a star, I noticed it right away. To the west, a bright white light was motionless in the sky. It started getting brighter and it started pulsating. So I pointed the video camera at it, put the camera in infrared mode, and started to film.

This happened for a good 3 minutes. Then, all of a sudden, it came within one mile of where I was standing and hovered in midair a few hundred feet up, remaining stationary.

My first thought was: *This has got to be another UFO.*

Next the object shot in a southerly direction at an unbelievable speed, which put me in a state of disbelief. Later, while watching this on video, I was amazed—just as everyone else who watches it is.

By this time, I was thinking a lot about what I was actually seeing and filming. For some reason I just knew these appearances were not of this world.

Why was I seeing them?

What's behind these experiences?

I felt myself changing spiritually, mentally, and physically. My world was changing, too, and the people around me were noticing the changes. It was a relief that nothing negative had come from my experiences, or from what I was telling people, because I was starting to go public.

My major concern was that my family might think I was crazy. I didn't care about what the general public or other individuals thought; I knew what I was witnessing was unusual. I needed to have the support of my family during these life-changing events, and, fortunately, it was what I got.

My unbelievably caring mother and her husband were supportive. My Dad (who was a police officer for thirty-eight years) and his wife were supportive, as was my brother, which made all the difference, along with Gary, my best mate of twenty-five years, William, and a few others. This gave me the strength to go public and talk about these experiences.

Where I live, there was no UFO society I could turn to for information and advice. The only support I had was on the Internet, so there were really no professionals in this field I could meet with in person because of my location.

After these sightings, the news media got a hold of me and did a piece that was well received. The paper did a story, too, and I was really stunned by the support from the public.

After the sightings that occurred in October, I contacted the flight control tower about any radar hits around the time of the incidents. They replied by saying the control tower was shut around that time each night, which doesn't make sense because there are planes coming into Albury until late.

Now I don't even bother contacting them, because all the responses are the same, so it's just a waste of time.

This period was like a UFO flap over my house because it happened six times in one month. And as I said before, William witnessed the UFOs three times.

I could have witnessed it the sixth time, but when the UFO showed up, I was in the shower and William was out in my lounge room. "Poyda, its back," he yelled, to which I replied, "Tell them to piss off and come back another time; I'm in the shower." And that was exactly what it did! I couldn't believe it when he went back out to see the craft and it was gone.

At first, William was skeptical about the sightings, but he did say we were not seeing a plane or a helicopter, and that it might be a type of military aircraft. After the third time he saw it, he was starting to think it might actually be an alien spacecraft.

So he was another witness to what I was seeing, along with video evidence.

HERE IS AN EMAIL I SENT TO THE AUSTRALIAN AIR SERVICES ON Tuesday, the 19th of October 2010

Hi, Peter here from IFTT Australia, (Paranormal UFO Society).

Just wondering if you could please tell me if you had any unusual air activity or helicopters flying into Albury (N.S.W.) at 20:00 hrs. from the southwest on the 17th of October 2010. Any reply would be much appreciated.

Thank you.

P.M Slattery.

IFTT founder

THE AUSTRALIAN AIR SERVICES REPLY:

Dear Peter,

Thanks for the inquiry. At the time in question, our air traffic control tower at Albury had closed for the evening, as per published hours of operation, so we're not able to provide any information that would assist in identifying the aircraft or other object in question. Sorry we could not help in this instance.

Regards,

Senior Adviser External Communication

CHAPTER 5

GHOST HUNTING

After the UFO flap over my house, it was time to go on a ghost hunt. It was late October 2010 and by this time I had done a few investigations.

SAMMY'S HOUSE

In the situation described next, I was asked to investigate a house in Myrtleford, which is located in the Alpine District area in Victoria, about an hour away from Albury.

The person who owned the house was a man by the name of "Sammy." He contacted me to investigate his house because he thought it might be haunted. He was having some experiences around the house that were unexplainable. He wanted my opinion on the situation. As soon as I arrived, Sammy described his experiences and showed me an E.V.P he recorded in the house on one of those voice activation digital recorders.

E.V.P stands for "electronic voice phenomena." To catch one, simply turn on a digital recorder and ask questions. Then, when you replay it, you might hear something that you didn't hear at the time, something unexplainable, like the voice of someone who wasn't physically present.

It was an active house, with reports of electrical appliances spontaneously turning on and off, the volume going up and down on the stereo for no apparent reason, and the sighting of a full-blown apparition by Sammy's mother, when visiting on one occasion.

Sammy had only just moved into the house, but he kept waking up to someone or something in his room. He could hear the sound of shuffling around and heavy breathing.

He also had similar experiences all over the house. So one night he decided to leave the recorder on in his bedroom when he went to bed to see if he could catch anything on it—which he did.

The digital recorder had definitely caught something that sounding like breathing out air loudly. At first, I thought it might be Sammy, himself, but with all the experiences he was having, I thought it best to keep an open mind.

An Italian man had owned the house and lived there until he died. Sammy was only the second person to own it. He showed me around and pointed out the renovations he had done since moving in.

Finding this out, and then learning he had done renovations, made me think that something might be going on, because it has been theorized that when a location is being renovated paranormal activity can be stirred up, due to changes in the environment.

After setting up the gear and sitting down with him and his mother (she had come over to tell me about the apparition she had witnessed), we started to get major cold spots that we could follow around the house. It's said that cold spots are a sign that paranormal activity is present.

About an hour later, when we were in the kitchen and I was checking the equipment, I saw a full body apparition. I couldn't see the top half clearly because my focus was on the ground with the equipment, but I saw a "person" walk straight past me. It looked human, but it was see-through, almost like grey and white smoke.

I mostly noticed his shoes and legs. He was wearing trousers and leather shoes. I didn't tell anyone about this experience until later, after the investigation. Just like any investigation, I wanted to sit back and let the evidence speak for itself.

Next we had an experience that was witnessed by all of us.

Later in the night, when we were back in the kitchen, we started to hear knocking sounds coming from the bathroom, which was several feet away from the entrance to the kitchen.

At first, I thought it might be the pipes in the house, but then I realized something was actual knocking on wood and it was coming from somewhere nearby. I started to ask questions, hoping to get an answer—and that was what happened.

I asked whomever it was to knock three times if someone was there. I heard three knocks in response.

Then I repeated the question twice and got the same response both times.

Next I said, "Knock once for 'No', and three times for 'Yes' in reply to my question if you would like to communicate. Then we heard three knocks. We were now clearly in communication.

I asked if we were communicating with a man, and he knocked three times to indicate, "Yes."

When I asked if he had a problem with Sammy living in the house, we got one knock back to indicate "No."

Then I asked if we were in his former house, to which he replied, "Yes."

After that I asked him not to scare the crap out of Sammy anymore, and that Sammy didn't mind him being in the house.

This helped Sammy realize he wasn't going insane and his experiences were real. It felt good to give Sammy peace of mind. Also, it put his mum at ease, after I told her I had seen the apparition, too.

All in all, my experiences at Sammy's house were amazing. Similar events are still happening.

OVENS DISTRICT HOSPITAL FACADE

Well...a month went by and it was time to move on to another investigation. This time I invited Sammy to come along. When we did the investigation at his house, he had shown an interest in going with me in the future. *Why not?* I thought. So I gave him a call, and that was that.

The next investigation was on the 30th of November 2010 at the old Ovens District Hospital Façade, which is in Beechworth. I had received many reports about this location having paranormal activity, so I thought I would take a look.

Beechworth has a lot of history; it was an old gold mining town, and at one time it housed the famous Australian Bush Ranger "Ned Kelly."

The Ovens District Hospital Facade was the main hospital in the area from 1857 to 1940. It eventually got pulled down for reuse of its material during World War Two.

Many people died at the hospital during the time it was operational. Today the front limestone wall of the building still stands with a huge beautiful lawn behind it.

Sammy and I witnessed amazing activity at this location. It was raining lightly the night of our investigation. When we arrived, first we did an E.M.F sweep. Everything was safe. I knew the hazards in the area because I had done a pre-investigation of the site.

While investigating, we witnessed people talking; it sounded like a group of men, but nobody was physically there.

Sammy and I decided to split up. He went into the next room, which was separated from me by a stonewall. After he had been in the room for about two minutes, we both heard a girl scream.

Sammy was like, "Did you hear that" and I was like, "Yeah."

When I rejoined him, he pointed to where the scream had come from. So I aimed my infrared video camera at that area and walked over to it. A white light appeared, came straight at me, and then disappeared!

It was a rush but it also scared the crap out of me!

Just after this experience, the rain started to get heavy and it was time to leave, but I was happy because we had a few experiences and caught one of them on the video camera.

The weather probably had a huge part to play that night in bringing on the ghostly activity, because it was humid and raining. It is theorized that a humid environment, or an environment with rain or electricity in the air, can help the spirits manifest.

It is also theorized that heaps of underground creeks and rivers with running water, and certain types of rocks and minerals such as quartz and gold, can also help spirits manifest because they add energy to the environment.

So the conditions were good for ghost hunting, because there are underground creeks, lots of gold, quartz, limestone and minerals in the land around Beechworth. Plus it was raining and humid.

After this experience, my drive to continue ghost hunting was upped. Also, Sammy continued to come on investigations with me and became part of IFTT. Looking for ghosts is a rush, and delving into the unknown made me even thirstier for knowledge.

BACK TO BEECHWORTH

On the 16th of December 2010, I did a private investigation at the Beechworth Asylum. Sammy lined it up to give us something interesting to do until another case came along. We ended up having some amazing experiences.

That night, we got a lot of knocking back when we asked questions. I was also dared to go into the infirmary by myself, which I did. Eventually,

Sammy came in and we got some E.M.F spikes for reasons unknown.

I saw a shadow man that night, which I assumed I caught on camera, but the camera had lost power. This is not unusual when ghost hunting, because it is theorized that when a spirit is trying to manifest, it can use the energy from the camera battery and also human energy to enable manifestation.

Outside the infirmary there is an area where patients had been kept in rooms only slightly bigger than a bathroom. This area was said to be very active. Nothing happened when I was there, but I found scratch marks and bite marks on the big thick wooden doors.

It was a rush to be in this area—and upsetting at the same time. To know that rape, violence, and pain were a major part of this place was sickening.

Beechworth Asylum was crazy back in the day. It opened in 1867 and closed in 1995. One of the Superintendents was even crazier than the patients! He once threw a lady out of the second story window in his office because she brought him the wrong smokes.

While investigating the bathroom area, I felt like I was spinning. The tour guide said a few days before the same thing had happened to a lady in the exact same spot. This was our only experience in that area.

People had been chained up in the basement, bodies were buried in the walls, and they also used to feed the patients laxatives so they wouldn't have time to be violent towards themselves or others.

Things picked up as the investigation continued. We got some activity in the infirmary, where it is said that over nine and a half thousand people died. It was a freaky but fascinating experience.

I saw a shadow man running around, which, as I said, I thought I caught on camera but the power had run out. We also got some high E.M.F readings in that area, and even more to back up the experiences, because there had been no electricity in the infirmary building for many years. This meant there was no reason for the high E.M.F readings.

This area was also wild. There was a medical treatment room where they extracted teeth without using painkillers. Some of the patients used to bite others, and if they kept on doing it, their teeth were pulled.

I highly recommend that anyone interested in ghost hunting visit the Beechworth Asylum, even if it's just for a tour. The Beechworth Jail does tours too.

Just remember, if you have love in your heart you will always be safe, because love is more powerful than most people believe.

Not all beings are good, so bad things can happen, things that can terrify you. Also, not all spirits were once human, so unless you know what you're doing, or you have an experienced ghost hunter with you, be extra careful.

As I said before, some ghosts are not aware they are being observed. This is the case in a residual haunting. So until you know what you dealing with, have respect. It will be helpful just in case you come across a location that has an intelligent spirit capable of interacting with you.

CHAPTER 6

REMOTE VIEWING, UFOS, AND PSYCHIC ALIENS

Around the end of 2010, I became even more involved with UFOs and other paranormal subjects. I bought books, DVDs, and even started taking a remote viewing course.

Remote viewing is viewing a distant place anywhere in space and time without physically being there. A specific type of protocol is used.

Physicists Harold Puthoff and Russell Targ, who were parapsychology researchers at Stanford Research Institute (SRI), are though to had created the term "Remote Viewing", though some say it was first called that by Ingo Swann who was part of their team and apparently highly psychic.

The course I took was on a DVD and the instructor was Major Ed Danes, who actually participated in the U.S. Army remote viewing program. These programs are done over a period of a few weeks, depending on how you progress.

Now...let me tell you. I was skeptical, at first, about the subject of remote viewing, but I can say now that it is real and anybody can do it. The key is to not think about it. As soon as you engage your thoughts, you can lose sight of your target, the object, place, or person you intend to view.

Following a specific protocol is required. First, find someone to get a picture of the target you want to view, and ask the person to draw a line to the object and designate it with two sets of four-digit numbers. Then have the person put the picture in an envelope, write the target number on the outside of the envelope, and then get them to give it to you.

Write down the target number on a piece of paper, or template, and do a squiggle after it. This is known as an "ideogram." Now go to work.

You are not allowed look at what is inside the envelope, because it would defeat the purpose of doing the exercise—unless you're doing a "front loaded session." In a front loaded session, you are allowed to see the target first.

As soon as you see a color (or colors), textures, or shapes, write it down (as the protocol says), along with whatever you smell and your feelings are. Basically what you feel or comes to mind you write down when going through your five senses, using your extrasensory perception abilities, better known as psychic abilities—which we all have. When doing this exercise, you don't have to be an artist, either.

Also mark with an "X" whatever you feel is the target, or the most important thing about it. There is a bit more to this exercise, but I'm just trying to explain the basics of it. If you are interested, I recommend doing a course. Remember...you will only get results if you really want to succeed. You must have the desire to do it.

Around this time, I also started to learn mediation, which later led to finding out that I could remote view that way, too. It took many different styles of meditation to find out what worked for me. But this is part of the process. It's all about what works for each individual.

A lot of practice is needed to get results. You need a strong desire to do remote viewing. It's all about self-development.

Remote viewing and meditation helped me deal with anxiety and opened my mind to a world of limitless knowledge. I learned to become one with the universe, so to speak, and how to tap into the universal consciousness that is all around us—and of which we are all a part of.

So now I was a man on a mission. I had witnessed a few UFOs and had a few paranormal experiences. I was looking everywhere for answers. After the paranormal experiences during my ghost hunting investigations, I was even more pumped than ever. Next I got some really good evidence.

On the 8th of March 2011, just before 2:00 p.m. in the afternoon, for some reason, I had an overwhelming urge to go outside with the camera and look up at the sky. My world was changed dramatically by what I captured on film.

This particular incident was weird. When I walked out the back door and looked north, there it was: a metallic UFO slowly hovering west.

I was absolutely blown away by this sighting. It was easy to spot, but to keep sight of it was hard. I don't know why. Maybe because it was a bit after midday and it was really bright outside.

Coming to my senses, I got my camera and took a photo. After that the UFO just continued on its way, going west. As soon as it had come, it disappeared.

Now…lights in the sky are one thing, but seeing a metallic, disc-shaped object during the middle of the day is a totally different and expansive experience. This has not happened to me just once, but many times. I have caught many UFOs on camera during the daytime.

On the 24th of March 2011, I was stargazing with my telescope again on a clear, beautiful night, when an object appeared north from my front lawn just over a quarter of a mile away. The object looked similar to a diamond. I had never seen anything like it, before or since.

I witnessed it hover for about 10 seconds and then it slowly moved away. I was able to get a photo of the craft, too.

It happened so quickly that I really didn't believe what I had seen until I looked at the photo. Then it sunk in. This was overwhelming evidence, from the point of view that I was able to view the object clearly and realize it was different from any of the other crafts I had witnessed up to this point.

This made me think even more about what was controlling these crafts.

Now I was on a mission, even more than before, to find out what was going on. The fact that I had witnessed these crafts so many times seemed like more than a coincidence. I was filming them at night and during the day, so something didn't seem right about the situation.

I was almost getting to the point of being aggravated, because I needed to know the purpose behind the sightings. I also needed to know why I was seeing them. I knew there had to be a reason, but what? It was overwhelming and

I had no one to turn to except myself. This helped me to trust, learn, and get to know myself better. I learned to trust my inner thoughts and gut feelings about what was happening.

My experiences were getting really trippy and it was out of my hands. So all I could do was try to be positive and think everything was happening for a reason, and that maybe one day the reason would be revealed to me.

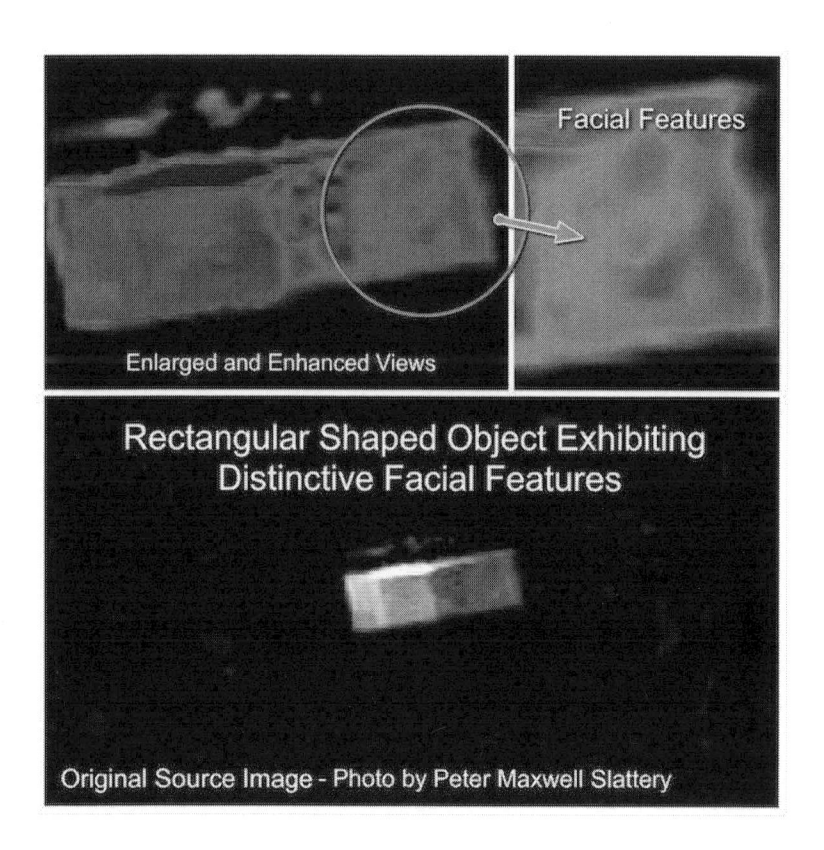

This is a photo of the 24th of March 2011 UFO analyzed by Jason Gleaves.

A couple of weeks later, I was sitting at home on the night of the 29th of March 2011, when all of a sudden I had an urge to grab the infrared camera. For some reason I felt compelled to put it on record and position it looking out the front window of my house.

I don't know why I did this. I had never done anything like it before, but the urge was so strong it was impossible to ignore. After leaving the camera facing out the front window for over 20 minutes, I pulled it down.

I didn't notice anything at the time, but on the video you can see the same UFO from some of my other experiences in the same location doing the same maneuvers. Furthermore, this footage goes for over 5 minutes.

I was just amazed at what had been captured on the video, and I wondered why I had felt an urge to put the camera in the window. It was shocking and unbelievably exciting —all in a positive way. After the research I had done, I was starting to wonder if I was receiving telepathic communication and not realizing it.

If not for doing remote viewing, I probably would have blown off the idea as soon as it came up. It was odd that on two occasions, when I had an urge to get the camera, I was able to film or take a photo of a UFO.

CHAPTER 7

THE MONTE CRISTO HOMESTEAD

It was time for another ghost hunt, so I booked a night for Sammy and me to investigate the most haunted house in Australia: The Monte Cristo Homestead, located outside of Junee in the state of New South Wales. Going somewhere that had produced so much evidence of paranormal activity was exciting!

The Homestead is advertised as a haunted bed and breakfast, and ghost tours are held for visitors. It was built around 1876 and was originally owned by Mr. Crawley, who was a very wealthy man.

Monte Cristo means "Mount of Christ." The Homestead is actually two houses joined together. Mr. Crawley lived in the first house until the second one was built, and then he and his family moved over to the newer house, which is bigger and better. Eventually, the two houses were joined. There are stables and a ballroom, as well.

The investigation took place on the 12th of May 2011.

As soon as we arrived, we had an experience in the horse cart display room behind the ballroom; this was later validated by others who had an experience there, too.

Photos of apparitions had been taken at this location in previous years, but we didn't know about this until later. These previous photos show apparitions and orbs in the same spot.

While we were in the room behind the ballroom, something was making the sound of footsteps walking around right in front of us. We couldn't see anything visually, but you could feel from the energy of the room that something was there.

Another weird bit of information is how the present ballroom came to be. The original ballroom had been knocked down years before the current owner, Reg Ryan, bought the property. But Reg wanted a ballroom so he built one.

Now it gets even weirder.

One day, a person who came to visit the Homestead said, "I see the ballroom is brick now."

"What do you mean?" said Reg. The person told him the ballroom used to be made of timber.

When Reg looked at the records of the house, it showed that a ballroom had been there. This former ballroom had the same dimensions as the one Reg built, and his new" ballroom was located in the exact same spot as the older one from years before. Reg found this out after his conversation with a visitor.

Reg later said that he felt he had been contacted subconsciously about rebuilding the ballroom. He also said he had the same feeling about buying the Homestead.

Even more amazing is that the whole time Reg has lived at the Homestead, he has never had a paranormal experience. His wife and three grown-up children have, and it continues to this day for his wife and kids whenever they pop by the house.

After dinner that night, before things got going, we watched a DVD about television appearances related to Monte Cristo. While watching this DVD, Sammy and I and one other person witnessed a white light go from one end of the building to the other end. This happened at the gift shop out in front of the Homestead.

Straight after, Reg's son, Lawrence Ryan (who holds a few world records for motorcycle stunt riding), asked us if we had seen anything unusual. "Yes" we replied. He said he had just witnessed the whole event on the security cameras.

We waited for everyone to go to bed so we could investigate the property privately—everyone stays in the new house, which is joined to the old one. We couldn't do all the rooms, but we had a number of other places to investigate that would not be contaminated. The place is gigantic.

When the investigation started, we first went out to the stables and the ballroom, which are located in the same place, away from the main house with some other buildings.

While we were at one of the stables, Sammy had a weird experience. We were just sitting down to do an E.V.P session, when he started getting hot sensations all over his body, to the point that he had to leave.

We later realized that this might have been connected to the little boy who was burned in the stable, and who later died in hospital. It happened because the boy was sick and couldn't get out of bed to work for the day. So Mr. Crawley threw a match on a bale of hay in his room, which was in the stables, and then locked the door. When we reviewed the E.V.P we got a scream and a noise like wood burning, similar to a campfire, which we didn't hear at the time.

Sammy caught another E.V.P that night, out in front of the house on the steps after everyone had gone to bed except us. A girl could be heard saying, "I'm serious, leave here." We didn't hear this at the time either, but I did get a weird feeling out there while doing the E.M.F and E.V.P sessions.

We linked the voice to a 15-year-old girl who was apparently thrown off the second story balcony and died on the steps out the front of the house, which is where the E.V.P was caught.

It's said that Mrs. Crawley threw her off the second story for having sex with her husband. Also, another girl the same age died on the second story after giving birth to Mr. Crawley's child.

Out in front, people have also reported seeing ghost children, but we got no evidence of this during our investigation.

That same night we met Tom, who also got some good evidence.

Now...Tom caught a few E.V.Ps during the day before the night tour. His specialty was doing E.V.P sessions. During one of his sessions, he asked if anyone wanted a drink, and he got a response from an unknown voice saying, "grape juice."

He got another response when he asked if anybody was in the room with him. The reply was a voice from an unknown source saying, "I'm a Gillespie." The next day when he told Reg, he found out that someone named "Mr, Gillespie" had built the houses for Mr. Crawley. What a trip! Mr. Crawley has also been seen on the grounds from time to time, as well. Unfortunately we didn't get to see him that night.

I saw some orbs and objects moving in the night sky, but I have no evidence to back it up.

Investigating Monte's was a fantastic experience. It's a beautiful old place with a lot of history. I recommend it to anyone and everyone. I won't say any more because I don't want to ruin it for you, in case you visit in the future. It's a must.

CHAPTER 8

REMOTE VIEWING, MEDITATION, AND THE BLUE GUY

I continued doing remote viewing and meditation, and eventually I had practiced so much that I could go right into the "zone" without even trying.

I don't talk much about my remote viewing experiences, and I don't do it in front of anyone unless a close friend or family member gives me a target just for fun, or to show them how it's done.

Usually they cut something out of a magazine and write a target number on it, and put it in the envelope with the target reference number on the outside. Then they ask me what the target is and I go to work. Anybody can do it.

As I said, around this time I was getting better at remote viewing and working with a lot of targets to satisfy personal curiosity; for example, "Who built the pyramids?"

And, yes, I have remote viewed the inside of UFOs. For some reason, I was only seeing a white light, feeling a presence, and hear nothing but silence at this time.

After many hours of practicing remote viewing, I started viewing locations on Mars and the Moon, and from there continued to expand out into the universe. In the process, I learned much about our hidden human abilities.

It was getting easier and easier to get into a meditative state and remote view using meditation, but with a lot more effort I was able to put my consciousness wherever I wanted to go. Things started to appear so clearly, but that wasn't the only trippy thing that happened, when I was remote viewing during meditation—or what some people call "astral traveling" and/or an OBE (out-of-body experience).

What I found was astonishing and I can understand what it must be like for you to read this, unless you already know about the paranormal. I kept seeing a blue being that seemed to be looking out for me. That's right, a blue being.

Remote viewing is difficult for most people to comprehend, so I don't expect everyone to believe what I say about the blue being, or about how I developed remote viewing skills naturally during meditation.

Seeing the blue guy was life changing and overwhelming, at first. I can't describe fully the way he looks or the feeling of love and peace that emanates from him. I get shivers up my spine just writing about it.

He appears to be a human with blue skin and black hair. He is really tall and fit, with a thin build. Somehow I know the being is a male, not just from appearance, but from the feeling I get from him.

What I remember most, from the many times I've seen him, is how big and black his eyelashes are. They are really thick and long. Also his eyes are so white around his royal blue pupils. Another thing is that he has long hair and pointy ears.

He wears no garment on top, but he does have some sort of black shorts or a cloth wrapped around the lower part of his body. He also carries with him what appears to be a golden spear.

I believe the blue man watches out for me when I'm remote viewing. I'm not entirely sure who or what he is, but I can tell you he's real. He sort of looks like the blue beings from the *Avatar* movie but different. This is the best way I can describe him.

After seeing him so many times, I consider him to be one of my unseen friends. He doesn't bother me, scare me, or anything like that. He just appears and follows me when I'm remote viewing in a meditative state.

Is he my protector, a guide, or is he around to make sure I don't access information that I shouldn't? I don't know, but what I do know is that he causes no harm. Only enlightenment has come from my experiences with the blue guy.

I am able to handle this alternative reality, because when mediating I'm in a dream-like state and things can be faint. However, some things are so clear, clearer than the reality we live in and think we know.

CHAPTER 9

GHOST HUNTING AND THE HUME HIGHWAY UFO

The next ghost hunt was on the 8th of April 2011 in Williamstown, which is located on the west side of Melbourne. The Time Ball Tower, the Morgue, Lavender Lane, and the Portal are some of the locations I investigated in Williamstown, which dates back to the 1840s.

THE PORTAL

Sammy and I conducted an investigation with Andrew, our tour guide. It was a very interesting night. We met at a pub and then headed down to an old alleyway that is known in the paranormal community as "The Portal."

Now...the Portal is in an old lane located in Williamstown. The lane was an area that everyone had to walk through to get anywhere, sort of the main part of the town back then.

It's said that if you tune into your senses when you are in the Portal, you can still hear the horses and buggies pass by and other sounds of the town from when it was founded by the white man.

THE LAVENDER LADIES

Nothing happened for us in the Portal, so we went to Lavender Lane, which is also an alleyway. It's now located at the side of a shop. The Lavender Ladies used to hang out there and sell themselves. This is why they call it "Lavender Lane." It's said they called the women there the "Lavender Ladies," because they didn't shower much—they used lavender as a deodorant.

This location was amazing. We were there for about ten or so minutes, and took our time doing some E.V.P work and E.M.F readings. Andrew asked if any of the Lavender Ladies were present while Sammy and I absorbed the location.

After some time, we started getting noises right in front of us. It sounded like footsteps, but nobody was physically there. The noises seemed to be happening for no reason at all.

Next we experienced the strong smell of lavender, which surprised us, because no one in the tour was wearing lavender, and it was just a plain old alleyway. After a few minutes, the noises and lavender smell went away, once we finished doing the E.V.P session. We caught nothing on the digital recorder, but we did have a fascinating experience.

TIME BALL TOWER

Then we went to the Time Ball Tower, which was built in the 1840s. The Tower is located right on the water and has a very brutal history. The convicts here used to dig the blue stone from around the tower, and apparently the people who ran the camp treated them very badly.

The head person who ran the prison camp at one time died in hospital after being attacked by convicts at the Time Ball Tower. It's believed he still haunts the Tower.

We went into the Tower to investigate and ended up catching something on the video recorder, but we couldn't make it out, even though we heard it at the time. It was a response to our asking whether there was anybody in the Tower. This was followed by the sound of someone, or something, shuffling around.

THE OLD WILLIAMSTOWN MORGUE

When we got to the Morgue, the action basically started straight away. Andrew was going on about how it feels like someone is always there to greet you at the door when you arrive.

Sammy walked straight up to the front door and knocked on it three times. He held the E.M.F meter up and got three knocks back with the lights lighting up in time with each knock. He did this three times as I filmed.

When we got inside, we saw it was just one room built out of stone bricks. We ended up knocking on the door from inside the Morgue and got the same result.

Next...the E.M.F meter kept red lining when we asked questions. We didn't get anything on the digital recorder, but I did film the whole experience.

I believe the morgue might have paranormal activity, based on the readings we were getting, which were responding in time to our questions by using the method of getting the spirit to light up the E.M.F meter twice for "no" and once for "yes" in response to our questions. We had asked the spirit to communicate in this way.

I really enjoyed the experience and the history of the town. If you're into this type of thing, I highly recommend it.

ALTONA HOMESTEAD

A month went by and we had our next investigation booked. It was time to get the car packed and get on the road.

It was the 10th of June 2011 and I had an investigation lined up at the Altona Homestead located in Altona, which is on the west side of

Melbourne, three and a half hours from my hometown. So it was a big drive.

It was dark by the time we arrived, which was perfect timing. So we got out the gear and got to it.

The Altona Homestead used to be occupied by the Langhorne family. It was built in the mid-1800s and it is said a little girl died there. The house was amazing and the history of the place is lengthy. It was once used for business and local government, then public housing, and finally the town council used it for meetings.

It has been preserved and it's open for daily tours. Once a month, they sponsor a ghost tour.

There have been claims of paranormal activity at the Homestead. The reports are everything from objects moving to apparitions. So I was pumped and excited to get out the gear and start investigating.

We didn't have much luck with E.M.F hits or E.V.Ps, but what we did come across was some shadow man activity in the back lounge room. This happened multiple times, and it was not just witnessed by me, but by Sammy, too. The night went smoothly.

Also, while I was sitting on the bed in the main bedroom, it started to shake. This has been reported multiple times, and luckily I was able to witness it for myself. But after that nothing else of interest happened—until we were packed and ready to go.

We were in the kitchen, picking up our bags to leave and saying good-bye to Jenny, who leads the tours, when something totally crazy happened.

For some reason Sammy and I decided to turn around, and when we did we saw a full-on mist in the corner of the room. The mist was expanding and growing. Sammy and I just looked at each other, like "what's that," and within another 10 seconds or so, it disappeared. We were shocked.

We asked Jenny if she had seen the mist, but she hadn't, because she was occupied in the kitchen cleaning up. If Sammy and I had been able to speak up sooner, she might have seen it, too.

POINT COOK HOMESTEAD

On the 29th of July 2011, we had our next ghost hunt. It was a big day; we drove 230 miles from Albury to Point Cook, which is located on the west side of Melbourne. Then we drove 230 miles back, just like the other investigations we did that were in Melbourne.

We were booked for a private investigation at Point Cook, because there had been many reports of paranormal activity there. When we arrived at the location, first we saw a café that backs onto a few paddocks. This leads to the popular "Point Cook Homestead."

This place dates back to 1857 and has a reputation for a lot of paranormal activity. Two brothers, Thomas and Andrew Chirnside, owned the property for many years, but that was a long time ago.

Thomas was to marry a girl named Mary, but first he had to get Mary to Australia from Scotland. Thomas sent his brother Andrew over to Scotland to pick her up. But when Andrew came back, he had already become romantically involved with

Mary. Andrew and Mary ended up moving into their own homestead nearby.

It's said Thomas haunts the house with a broken heart. There are many reports of chairs being pulled out from under people, and a shadow man roaming the house.

Around the same time, a man named "Tommy," who helped take care of the horses, was found hanging from the stable rafters, dead. Some say this was payback for Tommy drugging a famous racehorse that ended up dying.

There was also an old cellar where some people were kept. For some reason, I knew about it and told Jenny, who again was our tour guide. "How did you know that," she said. I replied, "I don't know, but I just do."

The Point Cook Homestead had its own meat and dairy facilities. And it's located right on the beach, so the environment is quite beautiful.

Being so open, it was going to be a bit of a challenge to investigate, and also it was windy. Wind can affect the E.V.P.s obtained and contaminate them, but that's part of ghost hunting.

We started in the smoke room, because we had been told about activity there. I felt drawn to the room as soon as we started the investigation. I went to the table in the middle of the room, got out the digital recorder and the E.M.F meter, and started an E.V.P session.

As soon as we got into the investigation, the lights on the E.M.F meter went off, red-lining on and off to our questions. Whatever or whoever was responding to our questions with precision timing was using the E.M.F meter to communicate with us.

When reviewing the digital recorder, nothing was found, but it was surprising that the E.M.F. readings were so high and in time with our questions, which made it a possibility that something paranormal was going on, because it happened smack bang on time in response to our questions for around three minutes. Nobody was around except Sammy and me, and the power was off, so there was no reason for those readings.

Furthermore, we kept seeing a shadow man ducking and running around, and there were unexplainable noises constantly going on. It sounded like boots walking on the ground. All this confirmed what other people had reported experiencing at the Point Cook Homestead.

From the smoke room, we continued to cover the whole house. The activity continued and seemed to follow us.

After a while, it was quiet in the house so I went out to the stables to see if we could get any evidence or witness anything paranormal.

When walking in to the stables we could feel the energy. It was intense and very much an adrenalin rush. We went straight to the area where the man was hanged.

After waiting—which you have to when in this field because nothing happens on demand—things started to get active. For starters, we again began to get responses on time to our questions, with the lights lighting up on the E.M.F meter. This actually went on for around five minutes, so it was longer than the session inside the house.

Again, we were amazed. Every time we asked a question, it was just like talking to a person because the meter lit up on time—just like the timing of a physical person responding to a question.

The confusing thing about both cases that night is we didn't actually get confirmation of whom we were talking to, which is a common result in ghost hunting. Just like humans in a physical form, ghosts also play pranks, lie, and deceive others, but they can also tell the truth and be enlightening. It all depends on the being that has been contacted.

So...even though our responses were on time, we didn't know whom we were talking with. When we asked if we were talking to Thomas or Tommy from the stables, we got a response, but it wasn't like a yes or no answer because the readings were sporadic.

For example, we might ask, "Are you so and so," one flash for "yes" and two flashes for "no." But in these incidents we got many repeated hits. This might be the excited spirit saying *yes* or *no*, or it could be trying to get across to us who (or what) it actually was. Either way, we were left with questions because we didn't know exactly whom we were communicating with.

We got "Yes" answers to our questions: "Do you like it here? Is this your home? Are you a man? Do you mind all the people who come to visit this place?" The spirit did answer: "No" to our last question: "Do you mind us being here?"

Just remember, a spirit is just as interactive as any human being living in a physical form. So remember to treat them the same way you would like to be treated.

Yes, there are cases and evidence of sometimes violent apparitions or demons, or whatever you want to call them. But don't get your adrenalin rush mixed up with the feelings of a negative entity.

For example, you will get an adrenalin rush when you come across a spirit. But if it's negative, you will still get the adrenalin rush, but what comes with it is a negative vibe in the room.

So avoid feeling threatened unless you feel the negativity. In this case, tell the spirit you don't have time for negative crap. Then go back about your business. The spirit will be impressed that even though you can't see it, you can still feel it. If you can't handle something, get out.

Some will respond, but being positive will drive away any negative spirits most of the time. In some cases, this won't work because the ghost hunter's spirit isn't really positive, and the spirit can tell this and play with it.

Just like the living, respect the dead. When a negative spirit gets over it, it will move on to another place in space and time. Remember...there are intelligent and residual hauntings, and other beings that have never been in human form. So until you know what you are dealing with, don't make threats, just be cautious.

UFO ON THE HUME HIGHWAY

After the rush from this case, it was time to drive back to Albury from Melbourne. But little did we know we had more to witness.

I was driving the car with Sammy on the Hume Highway, heading back to Albury (which goes from Melbourne to Sydney), when all of a sudden I looked up into the night sky and noticed a bright white light. It was different from the stars in the sky and much too close. Plus it was not moving like any known aircraft.

Staring at it while driving, I thought, *Should I tell Sammy*? But he was dozing in and out of being asleep, and before I could say anything, the object literally shot up into space and disappeared.

Straight away Sammy said, "I think I just saw a UFO."

"Yeah, I've been watching it for a couple of minutes, but I didn't want to wake you," I said.

"It just shot off into space like in a movie," said Sammy.

This was cool, because now another person had witnessed what I have been witnessing. This made all the difference to me, because when you have more witnesses, it adds more validity to the experience.

The fact that this happened outside of Albury proved to me that something definitely was going on with these experiences, and there was a reason for them. The question remained: *Why was I being shown these crafts? Was something expected of me?*

Point Cook Homestead ended up being the last investigation I did with Sammy and under the paranormal society name IFTT, because what happened over the next few months changed my whole life.

Originally, I was only going to take a break, but everything had become too much. I needed to give some serious thought to my experiences. Sammy understood. We had some great times together and I will always remember the investigations we did.

CHAPTER 10

DAYTIME SIGHTINGS AND THE RED ORB

Soon enough, another incident occurred during the day on the 27th of July 2011. This day was just like any other average winter day in Australia. The weather was cold, the air was fresh, and it was sunny outside.

Similar to the way a few of the other sightings had happened, something told me to go outside. And just like the other sightings, it took a few minutes of staring up into the sky—wondering why I was outside and why I was supposed to look at the sky—to realize what was going on.

After letting my eyes adjust to the brightness of the sky, there it was: a grey metallic object hovering in the sky.

Now…during this incident, it only hovered for about 20 seconds, during which I was able to take two photos of it. One was taken in infrared, because the camera was already in that mode. The second photo was not, because I had turned off the infrared mode to get a 12-mega-pixel color photo. After I took the photos, the object moved west and disappeared.

I believe it had actually been there longer, because of my feeling to go outside. After this, I was convinced that my urge to go outside and observe a UFO was definitely intentional.

These events continue to this day. I might be driving out and about, or at home cleaning, on the computer, cooking a feed, watching T.V, studying, or doing whatever, and something will tell me to go outside and look up at the sky. Then I see a UFO.

I have come to believe that whoever or whatever is controlling these crafts has psychic ability and technology far beyond our own. I have the feeling that they (whoever they are) know I am aware of them and they are giving me messages to go outside.

THE RED ORB AND "MISSING TIME"

On the 5th of August 2011, a red orb visited me! It happened so quickly, but luckily I caught it on video.

I went out to the backyard with the video camera and placed it on the table, facing up towards the sky, and put it on record. Then I sat down and looked up into the sky.

All of a sudden, I saw a red light come over my head from the west and go east. Then it came back and went east again. The next thing I knew I was inside and waking up the next day! I couldn't even remember how I got inside. Then I remembered seeing the red orb.

The night before, my brother was coming to town and I was supposed to visit him at my mum's house—but I didn't show up. I remembered being outside seeing the red object, and then waking up inside the house the next morning, with no recollection of where I'd been or what happened.

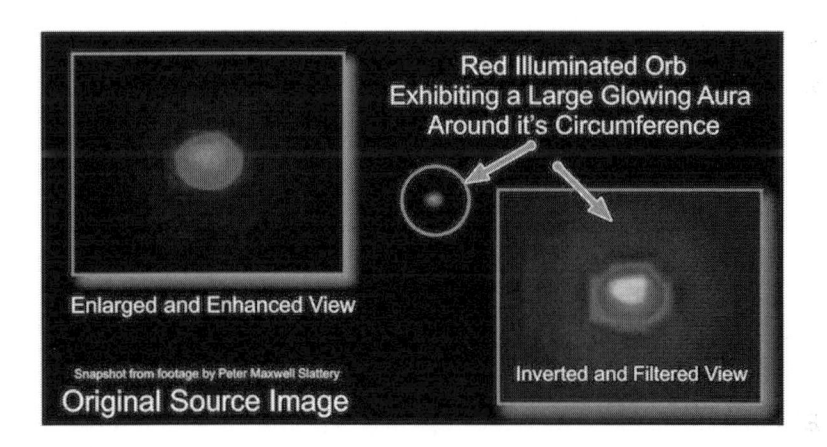

This is a snapshot from the video of the "Red Orb" analyzed by Jason Gleaves.

The next day, I checked the video. It captured what I had seen, but then the video just ran out until the end of the memory, with footage of the night sky for about another 20 minutes.

I didn't think much of it at the time, until later.

I had never experienced "missing time" that I could remember, up to this point, but it sure wasn't the last time I would have "missing time," either.

So the sightings were becoming more frequent, which freaked me out a bit. My main concern continued to be why.

Having no one to really talk to, and having nowhere to get answers, I got even more into the paranormal field to find out what was going on. This led to helping others deal with their experiences, even though I didn't know how to myself. I believe just talking and communicating with others in this field helps those who are in similar situations. It was hard on my family, too, and I hated feeling like a burden on them, even though they didn't see it that way.

Yes...here in Australia we have alien abduction groups and UFO societies, but being located between Melbourne and Sydney out in the rural area, made it impossible for me to talk to others who have knowledge in this area. It's not like America.

Australia has almost the same landmass as the U.S., but we have a population of twenty-three million. However, there are not as many people interested in the paranormal.

I am proud of the groups in Australia and worldwide for what they are doing, giving support where needed. But in my circumstances, I didn't have a support group or anyone else I could turn to. So I learned to deal with it on my own.

Not too long after my last experience, another one occurred. This time it was totally different. I didn't see one or two UFOs, but many.

On the 14th of August I witnessed a fleet of them in broad daylight for the first time. At least twenty to thirty UFOs flew over my house in a matter of about 20 seconds.

Feeling an urge to go outside, I grabbed the camera and went out back. It was a partly cloudy, partly sunny day, and there was an opening in the clouds. I looked up and, once my eyes adjusted, I saw them doing a fly by. It was a fleet of UFOs, not the disc type, but the round white craft type, just like the Brazilian and Mexican UFO fleets.

Who would have thought of this happening over a small city in rural Australia, right over my apartment?

Witnessing these crafts was thrilling and had a huge effect on me. I'm not sure why, because I had seen a few UFOs before. Maybe it was because there was so many of them. It was like they were reassuring me that I'm not crazy and my experiences are real.

Unfortunately, the picture I took of the UFO fleet was taken using infrared, because my camera was in that mode when I took the photo.

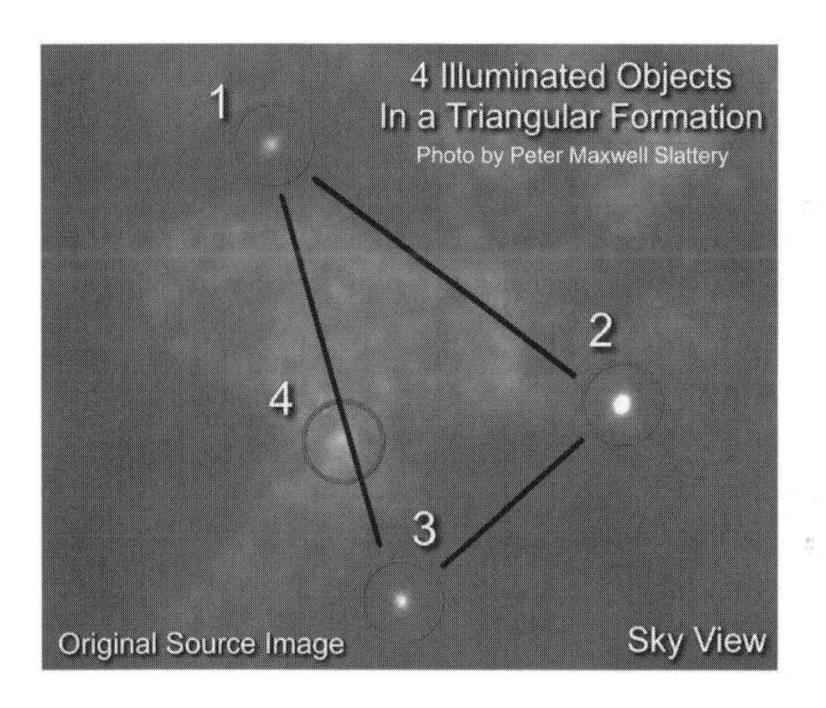

This is a photo showing part of the UFO fleet from the 14th of August 2011 analyzed by Jason Gleaves.

HEATHWOOD PARK, LAVINGTON

Another incident occurred around 2:00 p.m. in the afternoon at Heathwood Park in Lavington near my home on the 25th of August 2011.

It was a sunny day and I decided to go for a walk, as I often do, down to the park near my house. This park has a walking path with many trees and a creek.

About a quarter of my way through the walk, for some reason I looked up and there it was, a UFO.

At first, I thought it was a plane because of how white it was, but after a few seconds I realized it was hovering, stationary and not moving. After getting a photo of the craft on my phone, it seemed to disappear, or so I thought.

I continued to keep walking through the park and then got on the main road known as "Urana Road." I started to head home and when I was about two blocks away from my place, I saw it again.

Straight away I got out my mobile phone and used the camera on it to take a few photos and about 10 seconds worth of video footage. At first, it was hovering and then it flew over the main area of Lavington. Next it shot off to the north at an unbelievable speed.

Before I realized what was happening, I had another incredible experience. It felt like "they" were slowly easing me into some specific experience, because the sightings started to get even more frequent and closer.

This is a photo of the 25th of August 2011 UFO analyzed by Jason Gleaves.

CHAPTER 11

RED LIGHT HILL

It was the 1st of September 2011 and the weather was warming up. The nights were fresh and the skies were clear—perfect conditions to go up to "Red Light Hill" and look through the telescope at the stars, a favorite hobby of mine. Also it was not just a matter of wanting to go, something inside me told me I *had* to go.

I can remember this incident like it happened yesterday. It was about 10:00 p.m. and the conditions were right, so I headed up to Red Light Hill, just north of Lavington. You get a beautiful view of Albury and the stars up there at night.

Every now and then, when I go up Red Light Hill, I feel like I'm being watched. Usually, I imagine it's some kangaroos in the scrub, though sometimes I get a strong urge to take pictures. So I do.

It's a pretty big hill with huge television and communication antennas on it, a quarry, and a big red light so the planes in the area know where the hill is and can avoid flying into it.

The air was really electrified that night, like before a lightning storm. But there were no clouds in the sky; it was a very clear night.

After being up there for about 15 minutes, I noticed something that looked like a star. It was flying at the same height as an aircraft would fly. It was flying from west to north, and for a second I thought it was an aircraft, but then it stopped and remained stationary. It stayed still for about twenty seconds. *"That isn't a plane,"* I said to myself.

All of a sudden it continued on its way across the night sky—until I got out my flashlight and pointed at it. Straight away it stopped and I freaked out. When I did it again, the "light" moved slightly north and stopped again.

After pointing my flashlight at it a few more times, the light started to intensify and came directly towards me, until it reached the height of a low flying aircraft. Then it hovered for about

10 seconds. Finally it shot up to the path it was originally on at a high speed and disappeared.

At this point, I really started to get emotional. *This is not possible. I'd heard of people shining lights at a UFO and getting a reaction or response. But I didn't think it would happen to me.*

Now…I have to say…at the height of my freak-out, I think whoever or whatever it was could tell I was upset, because when I really felt scared the light went back to the height where I had first seen it, and then it continued on its way.

Not until I got home that evening did I think, *Damn, I had the camera out and I didn't even get it on film. No one will believe me.*

I didn't tell anybody about this incident until three or four months later. I was having a hard time absorbing what I had witnessed and needed time to process the experience.

The next day, I got out the camera to have a look at the photos I'd taken earlier the previous night, before I saw the UFO.

Now…I have been investigating the paranormal for a few years and have learned how to tell the difference between real orbs, bugs, and dust. What I found on the photos was not dust or a bug, in my opinion. I don't claim to know everything; I'm just connecting the dots from my own experiences and looking at the possibilities.

After this experience, I was still wondering why I was seeing UFOs. I knew it was not by chance or a coincidence.

Taking a photo of one, seeing one, yeah to most is a once in a lifetime thing, but now I was connecting the dots, which made me think how I could see apparitions, too, not just once but many times. I was seeing things not many people have seen, too often to count.

This is what led me to the decision that these events were happening to me for a reason. *Why?* I don't know for sure, but the number of times I have encountered UFOs and witnessed the paranormal makes it a possible explanation that has to be looked at. The evidence calls for it.

If I am crazy, then former U.S. President Jimmy Carter, military personnel, police officers, and people from every walk of life all over the world must be crazy, because these are the types of people who have also witnessed a UFO and have gone on the record about it.

Why me? I'm not special, but other people have told me that maybe these spirits and beings are open to me because I'm open to them. Who knows? But it's a possibility.

Soon I was feeling that something or someone was making me hold onto what I was experiencing in full detail until the right time, because so far only my family knew the full extent of my experiences.

Around this time, I had another UFO sighting while driving to see my brother in Bright, which is located in the Victorian Alpine District area.

I was between Myrtleford and Porepunkah, about 20 minutes from Bright, when I noticed a UFO in front of me, high in the sky over the Buckland Valley.

This thing was doing crazy maneuvers; I went to pull over so I could take a couple of pictures. As soon as I turned on the camera the object disappeared. I just had my second sighting out of Albury.

CHAPTER 12

THE BLUE ORB

After the last incident, I started to wonder even more than ever whether the orbs and crafts I was seeing were connected. I'm sure that some of the ghosts I had encounters with were once in human form. But I was thinking maybe something else was at play when I was ghost hunting.

I had known from day one, that the UFOs I was seeing were not human creations. We are a very intelligent race, but as far as I'm concerned these crafts are "not of this world." I started to think about how I was seeing orbs after and before UFO sightings, which I don't go on about much because I don't have any evidence.

This really played on my mind, because looking back you see and recognize things that you don't see at the time. Seeing orbs before and after UFO sightings has happened to me on many occasions.

Around this time, I had birds fly into my car a few times while driving around town. Even at work, while sitting down having lunch during the same time period, birds would fly straight into the window of the room where I was sitting.

I found out later this might be due to the energy around me. I had heard about some abduction cases, in which the birds and electrical appliances react or are drawn to this energy for some reason. This happened over a period of three days. After everything was quiet for about a month, I experienced another strange occurrence.

On the 14th of October 2011, a bit past 9:00 p.m., I was in my lounge room on the laptop, when I kept hearing a crackling and buzzing noise coming from the kitchen. This occurred for about five minutes, and I wondered: *What's going on?*

When I went to the kitchen, I saw a weird blue orb fly from the right side of the kitchen, straight through the kitchen window and out to the backyard. The only way I can explain this is to say it was like looking through 3D glasses, which made the light appear like some sort of hologram.

Straight away I grabbed the camera (keeping one nearby had became my habit) and ran out back. I looked around for a few seconds, until I noticed it again and took a photo.

Orbs are nothing new to me. I've seen a few, and I now believe they are beings in pure form between bodies, whether human or alien. It's what we are before and after death.

People say all the time that they see lights and orbs around me, including people in the paranormal field and people who don't even know what an orb is, but they describe it as a ball of light. At home, it happens more frequently, but I don't document it all the time. Even my E.M.F meters go off regularly for unknown reasons.

This incident with the blue orb was different, although I didn't put two and two together until recently, when I realized there is a connection between UFO sightings and black helicopters.

The day after this happened, for the first time I saw an unmarked black helicopter fly very low over my house. It flew around my place a couple of times.

I was sitting inside making a coffee when I heard the helicopter. I looked out the kitchen window and there it was. This thing was flying really low. There were no markings on it, and it just hovered around my place. I managed to get video footage of the incident. To tell you the truth, this incident tripped me out a bit. The same thing has happened a few more times since then.

I had heard of the black helicopter phenomena before, in which abductees, witnesses, and people involved in the UFO field have been monitored and intimidated by them, but I didn't think much about it until it happened to me.

The helicopter that flew over my house the first time could have been connected to the visitor from the night before—or it might not be. But I would not be surprised if I am being monitored, considering how open I am about the phenomena in public and how strange things frequently happen around me.

Having a visitor the night before and then experiencing a helicopter fly over my house made me wonder if I was being visited by inter-dimensional beings or beings from elsewhere without even knowing it.

The frequency of my seeing orbs, ghosts, and UFOs shows me that something bigger is at play here, but what?

After thinking about it, the possibilities were overwhelming. Then I realized it's impossible to know for sure, because all I'm doing is speculating.

To tell you the truth, I was intimidated by the black helicopter incident the first time, but later I realized there was no need to be scared. If something is going to happen, it's going to happen. It's a part of life that we can't control everything. So you have to roll with whatever occurs and just ride it out. That's my motto: "Just keep on riding."

CHAPTER 13

VISITED BY A LIGHT BEING

The next happening was even more dramatic than my previous encounters of the paranormal kind.

It was the 4th of December 2011. Summer had kicked in, and it was time to stay inside and chill out under the air-conditioner.

I was watching television, just chilling, when all of a sudden, basically in the middle of my lounge room, a light appeared. This thing was incredibly bright, yet I could look directly at it. At first, I thought it was an orb, but then realized it was a being in human form. It was about seven feet tall and made entirely of blue light.

It had vague features resembling a head, mouth, ears, nose, neck, and a body, along with two arms and two legs, but nothing was defined. It was like a ghost but totally different.

It had hair, too, but there was no difference between the hair and the body parts. It was all one and the same.

It was a light blue color and white light was shining out from it all over the room. The way the light shone was like having a light blue light bulb, but the light you get in the room is white. It's really hard to explain.

Now…this being didn't say anything. It just stood there in the middle of the lounge room not even looking at me. It gave the impression it was absorbing the environment, taking it all in.

To tell you the truth, it didn't even scare the crap out of me. I was just in shock, thinking: *What's going on here?*

During this experience I had an overwhelming feeling of wisdom, power, authority, and love. I really can't explain it any other way.

One weird thing about the being was it also looked like a liquid, but it might have been just how the being, or how the light in the being, appeared. It's like this thing was made of light, literally.

After about 40 seconds or more, it simply disappeared. The only way I can explain the way it left is imagine you cut a frame out of a film. One minute it's there, the next minute it's not.

First I thought I might be having heatstroke, but it was the middle of the day just before lunch and it was around 68 degrees Fahrenheit inside.

It was not like anything I had previously come across in my paranormal investigations, but it was something that I had heard about in the UFO community. I now believe I witnessed a light being.

This incident left me with many more questions about what was happening to me, and the nature of reality and dimensions.

After this experience, I tried to put it in the back of my mind like the other apparitions and orbs I had seen, but it wasn't easy because the experience was so dramatic. Also it was not the last time I would see the light being.

CHAPTER 14

BEAM SHIP

My next sighting happened on the 14th of December 2011. It was the closest I had ever seen a UFO up to this point.

When in the lounge room, I again got the urge to go outside. So I grabbed my camera and went out to the backyard. There I saw a light about 46 feet long and around 6 to 10 feet in diameter. It looked like a cigar-shaped UFO. It was about 9:30 p.m. and the sun had just gone down. It was getting dark and the UFO emitted a very bright white light.

This thing appeared as a white light hovering in the air a couple hundred feet off the ground above a house a couple of doors down from mine. I had a perfect view of it from my backyard.

After a few seconds of taking in what was happening, I raised my camera and took a photo. Straight away after that it shot west and disappeared in about 2 seconds. I was in shock. This was as close as any UFO I had seen before, and it was not the classic UFO, nor was it the white ball type UFO you see in fleets.

After this incident, I sat in my home daydreaming about the UFO I had just seen. I had never seen anything like it up to this point. I was really in shock about how different it was. This craft was definitely not of our world.

Although it appeared like a cigar-shaped UFO, it was also like a long fluorescent light and it was really bright.

This wouldn't be the last time I would see it. About 11:00 p.m. that same night, I noticed a really bright white light coming in through the kitchen window. So I grabbed the camera and went outside to investigate.

The same craft was shooting away from my place at around a 45-degree angle into the night sky. Quickly, I aimed the camera at it and took a photo. Then it disappeared. This second sighting felt like a confirmation saying, "Yes! You did see this earlier."

Around this time I started to witness white vertical lights with jagged edges about 3 feet long hovering vertically around my house on the odd occasion. Later, I started thinking these lights could be otherworldly beings.

These experiences changed me more than ever. They were intensifying, and seemed to be leading up to something, which made me ponder more into metaphysics, spirituality, and anything and everything, from UFOs to ghosts.

Most people who witness what I have, usually only see a ghost or a UFO once, maybe twice. *Why was I seeing both frequently?*

Everything, up to this day, is still happening. The only problem is dealing with it personally. This is a battle in itself. Also I wondered: *Is the light being I saw earlier in the month connected to the UFO I witnessed twice in one night.*

For some reason I also got the feeling that this was happening to me so I could play my part in exposing the E.T and paranormal reality to others. Later I was to find out that I was right.

Life became spiritually, mentally, emotionally, and physically more intense over the following months. I was feeling many changes.

I was so alert that I could go straight into a meditative state. I was doing things and was aware of things that I didn't even know I knew. For some reason, I knew when things were going to happen. I felt really in tune with everything around me, *but why?*

It wasn't a bad thing. It's like you wake up in the morning and know all this stuff. Friends and family were saying, "It's like there is another person inside of you." And I had to agree.

With everything that had happened to me up to this point, I began to realize there was an important reason behind it; there was a purpose behind my experiences. It was playing on my mind all the time. I was obsessed, but soon my direction would change.

Emotionally, my paranormal experiences began to take a toll on me, and I had to stop investigating and stop taking UFO reports from others. *It was just too much.* I decided to concentrate on what had been and was still happening to me. This attitude allowed me to back off from dealing with the experiences of others. It's the only way I could continue looking for answers related to my own experiences.

After years of witnessing paranormal activity and UFOs, the questions that stuck with me were:

Why me?

Why am I seeing ghosts?

Who are these beings and orbs?

What do they want?

How did I know when to go outside?

Why am I seeing these things a lot more than the average person and able to catch them on film?

All these questions were on my mind constantly. And the only way I could get answers was to just wait and hope that one day I would find out.

This was what happened. The answers would come in a form I could never have expected. The next few months would be the most exciting and intense time in my life, even more than all of my previous experiences put together.

PART TWO

MEETING SHI-JI

CHAPTER 15

THE VISITOR

On the 1st of January 2012, the first day of the New Year, I felt like I was going to have a mental breakdown.

The night before, New Year's Eve, I didn't drink. Actually, I very rarely drink alcohol anymore. Also I had become a hermit and shut myself off from the outside world. After everything that had happened, there was nowhere to go for help and no one to talk to. Then, just when I thought things couldn't get more intense, they did.

It was still light outside, about 7:00 p.m., and I was moping around the house asking the questions we all do when we feel down: *What's the meaning of life? Why is this happening to me?*

All of a sudden, a beautiful female appeared in the middle of my lounge room. She was leaning over my coffee table, crouched over with her hands on her knees, looking straight into my eyes.

At first, I was jolted backwards, in shock. The thought that came to mind was: *What's going on here? Am I dreaming?*

When I came to grips with the fact that this lady had showed up out of thin air, and I looked into her eyes, I realized she was not an average human. She had wavy, blondish brown hair, and her skin color was between that of a Caucasian and an Asian. Also she had huge blue eyes. They were bigger than human eyes. She was also very beautiful.

She was wearing a turtleneck type top, which was black from the shoulders up. The rest of her clothing, from her shoulders down, had patterns all over it: rectangles, squares, all sorts of shapes that were black, blue, and yellow in color.

The best way to describe the material of her garments would be to say it was similar to a wetsuit, but it was also different.

As she stared into my eyes, I experienced an overwhelming feeling of love. It felt like meeting a long lost friend.

When the fact of her arrival started to sink in, I asked her, "Who are you?"

"My name is Shi-Ji," she said—*but her lips didn't move*.

I asked where she was from. "The Pleiades," she said. (Pleiades is a star system.) So I asked her where it's located and she told me I would not understand.

When she stood up, she appeared to be the same height as me, around 5 feet 11 inches.

Before I could think of what else to say, she told me she communicates by thought, or as we would call it, "telepathy."

At this point, I was just trying to contain my emotions.

She told me to keep doing what I am doing, and that I don't know who I really am, yet. She then went on to say I'm more than I know now. When

I asked her what she meant, she said, "In time, Pete, in time."

Besides tripping out because she had appeared out of thin air, I also started to wonder: *How did she know my name?*

Next...she started talking about meditation, and how it could connect me to my real self and my mission on earth. She continued speaking about my purpose and how I have been accessing other dimensions through meditation, and that everything can be accessed by connecting with what I would call "universal consciousness," and that we are all connected, and that I know this, and I need to stop being stubborn and learn to trust what I feel.

She said these truths have been given through the teachings of Jesus, Muhammad, and the like, and that accessing this level of consciousness was lost knowledge, due to the teachings being changed and misinterpreted. They were all talking about the same "God Source, The Creator, The One," but the churches and other religious establishments had changed most of the teachings—because those in power wanted to control the masses and have power over the people.

"It's your assignment, along with many others, to get this knowledge back out to the people," said Shi-Ji.

She had more to tell me:

"Jesus, Muhammad, Ezekiel, and Mary are all real and they are Masters, which means they are highly-evolved beings. Humans grow in knowledge and enlightenment, and when they reach a certain point in their evolution they ascend, back to the God Source."

Shi-Ji continued: "Your experiences have served the purpose of awakening you because you are like the Masters, and because they are like me. We are all one and the same. Everything that has happened since your first sighting was planned to slowly awaken you and prepare you for The Shift that is taking place."

I asked her what she meant by The Shift, and she said, "It's a transformative event that will be more noticeable soon, and you will play your part. Everything up to this point was planned to awaken you at this time in need."

At this point, I was feeling a bit worried. "Will the people of earth be safe?"

"Yes, The Shift isn't going to happen the way most people think. Actually, it already started a few years ago."

Shi-Ji also said that she and others from her group, and many other groups, have and are contacting people like me all over the world for the purpose of raising the vibrational frequency of all the people on earth and the planet, itself.

She spoke about how her group's crafts and those of other groups are seen more often, because by being seen they can spark the flame in the minds of humans about earth not being alone, and that it's all about energy for those who are ready to be awakened.

"Even though you cannot understand all of the information I have transmitted at this time, keep to your present path, know everything will be revealed when the time is right for you, individually, and for each and every human being."

Then, all of a sudden, she disappeared!

The moment she vanished, I heard her voice in my head saying, "Come outside." So I ran out and there was one of the UFOs I had been seeing, just hovering around.

Straight away I ran inside and grabbed my camera and ran back out and took a photo. After that it disappeared.

What a trip. I felt like Shi-Ji was confirming my experience.

CHAPTER 16

AFTER EFFECT

I realized it was Shi-Ji's UFO outside, and that I had seen it before. Now I was getting answers. This was an absolute expansion of my understanding.

I went back inside, put the photo up on the computer, and just sat there looking at it, while absorbing what had just happened. It was a lot to take in.

Shi-Ji looks exactly like a human being, except for her eyes. They are gigantic.

The other thing to ponder is how she spoke to me in my head—this is really hard to explain. Her voice was clearer than a person speaking out loud. It's like her voice vibrated inside my head, bringing with it a feeling of love and giddiness.

How does she know how to speak English—and telepathically? How did she appear out of thin air?

Unless something like this has happened to you, it's hard to imagine the shock and wonder of it. There was so much to take in on many levels, and I felt so many emotions.

The things she said made me think about who I am, my path, and my purpose. *Keep doing what you're doing, she said, and Jesus and the rest are real and The Shift.* It's like she was speaking in riddles; at least that's how it seemed at the time.

I had not spoken telepathically to anybody up to this point. I knew nothing about it, only that a being not of this world had made contact with me. My mind was chaotic and in confusion.

Later the same night, something happened to put me at ease. It was a confirmation of the experience, as well as seeing and taking a photo of her craft.

Feeling absolutely drained, I was lying on the couch falling asleep when all of a sudden I heard Shi-Ji say, "It's alright Pete, it's okay."

Scared and shaken, I opened my eyes and sat up, but nobody was in the room with me. I got up and checked around the house, and still nobody was there. It seemed like she was confirming my experience was real and I was safe. The rest of the night, I felt restless, a bit upset and thinking about meeting such a beautiful being and how she appeared out of nowhere and spoke to me in my head.

* * *

Given that I had not lived with anyone for over four years, it was easy for my life to be taken over by these unusual experiences. Being alone gave me time to ponder on things and do a lot of soul-searching. When I wasn't thinking about my experiences, I was mediating.

Some people say, "How could you let UFOs take over your life." This type of question sometimes comes from people who have had experiences similar to mine. But I say to them, "Whether a person has been abused, abducted, or whatever, we all respond and deal with it in our own way."

Yes...up to this point seeing UFOs was a major event in my life, and it still is. But how I was dealing with it would soon change, because I no longer had the mindset of: *What is going on?*

What am I seeing? Who controls the UFOs I've been seeing?"

Now I knew I was experiencing otherworldly beings and their technology. Until a situation arises, you never know how you're going to deal with it.

The conversations in this book between Shi-Ji and me have been written as close as possible to what was actually said. Each time I saw her there was no way to record our conversation, and to tell you the truth this was the last thing on my mind.

When thinking about my UFO sightings later, it occurred to me that for some reason I always knew when to go outside and see a craft (which I wrote about in Part One). Now everything was different because Shi-Ji had come from The Pleiades to communicate with me.

Telepathically, it was a confirmation of my ability to "know" things, and having the courage to follow my gut feelings—which we all have. I believe this is what Shi-Ji meant when she told me, "Don't be stubborn."

When it happens, it first appears as a thought. In the beginning, when I thought I was being communicated with, I would go outside to look in the sky for a UFO—and one would be there. Now I know that when I had the urge to go outside, I was being contacted and directed.

This changed my whole perspective on what we are capable of as humans. I came to believe that we are all capable of experiencing telepathic communication with highly-evolved beings from other planets.

Yet...this wasn't all. More was going to happen over the next few months.

It's like when I thought I had an answer or knew something, something else would happen to put my last theory out of the mix. New information and experiences were being revealed slowly, which opened me up to more than I could have ever imagined about the nature of the universe. I learned that human life does not end, but rather we continue to gather knowledge and evolve.

My experience with Shi-Ji was so hard to deal with in the beginning, because I didn't know whom I could turn to. I didn't tell anyone about her for a couple of weeks.

Everything about Shi-Ji was so much to think about. I spent many days pondering what she said and the way she looked, with her eyes, her clothing, and how she could appear and disappear. And how she could speak to me telepathically. I wondered exactly where in The Pleiades Shi-Ji came from after doing some research.

It was an overload of a reality hit, coming all at the same time.

Besides all my new questions, I did get some answers to questions that had played on my mind for many years. Now I knew for certain who was flying the disc-shaped UFO.

I also learned for certain that humans have more senses than we have been led to believe, because I had received telepathic communications from an "otherworldly being," and vice versa. So besides my remote viewing experiences, I had discovered the ability to communicate by thought!

I also had confirmation that Jesus, and the other ancient Masters are real, and because of what Shi-Ji said about them, I understood they are all talking about the same "God Source." It was so satisfying to contemplate.

I believe humans mistook extraterrestrials for Gods, because they were so advanced compared to us. Personally, I already believed that Jesus, and many other people in most Scriptures from many religions were real, but that their teachings had been misinterpreted when transcribed into English—and that the teachings had been changed for man's own gain by those who were in power.

Hearing Shi-Ji say that Jesus and the other Masters are evolved beings proved to me that they are real.

I do believe in God, too, but not like everyone else. I believe God is greater than what most think, and that all of us are a part of God, and that as we become more highly evolved over many lifetimes, and as we gain life experiences in many forms, we evolve each time, growing with enlightenment and knowledge in each life. And eventually we reach a point where we go back to that which we came from, which is the "God Source," the Source of all.

Shi-Ji also spoke of something she called "The Shift." What's that about?

This talk of the Shift indicated to me that something is going to happen on a large scale, and that it is already in process. She spoke of how The Shift has been in play for a few years already. So something's going on, but what?

The questions that played the most in my mind were: *What does she mean that I don't know who I am? What does she mean by my being awakened, my purpose, and to get lost knowledge back out to humanity?*

The "why" had grown larger than ever before, including all of my previous paranormal experiences.

Then there was the fact that Shi-Ji appeared in the privacy of my own home, even though the doors were locked. She appeared out of nowhere, very much like a ghost, yet she looked as real as any living human being.

CHAPTER 17

PSYCHIC PREDICTIONS

Something totally unexpected happened on the 12th of January 2012.

Just for fun, I asked a highly respected psychic, who has been my friend for a while, to give me a reading over the Internet.

She told me months earlier, around mid-2011, that if I ever wanted a free reading she would do one. So in January 2012, I contacted her. I was curious about the unusual experiences I was having. I didn't expect much to come of it, but some of the information she revealed to me was totally unexpected.

The psychic was a lady from Nevada in the U.S. The first thing she wrote back to me in an email was that I have an overwhelming amount of energy, much more than the average person.

Then she said I have a very strong relationship with the universe and celestial and supernatural beings.

I didn't know what to think.

This started to trip me right out, but what she wrote next was even more food for thought. She said I have the same psychic ability she has, and if I studied and practiced I could do what she does. She told me to read her books on how to be a psychic if I was interested. Then she sent me all five of her books in pdf format, for free.

She said that recently I had gone through some life-changing experiences, and the next few months would bring even more changes. She said I would be writing my own books. I disregarded this comment at the time, because I had no interest in writing. She finished off by saying that doing a reading for me was overwhelming and draining.

The lady said she would like to get a few of her psychic friends to continue my reading at another time, and I said okay if that was what she wanted. I have to say, I wasn't totally impressed at the time. But I was later, because over the next few months, her predictions turned out to be spot on.

After a couple of days, she got back to me by email with information about what happened after she and the group did a reading about me. She said the group could not get any more information and that I have a lot of energy.

I told her that she had done enough for me and I was extremely grateful for her services and her time, and I left it at that.

I have to say, I was absolutely amazed by the information she offered, and that later it all turned out to be correct. At the time, I had just met Shi-Ji a week and a half before, and over the coming months I wrote three books.

It's weird how the universe works. I don't think this was all a coincidence. Yes…sometimes you have to question what people tell you, but this was too accurate to be taken for granted.

Also I found her to be legitimate because she didn't do the usual type of "reading." She merely said I have the ability to do what she does, and I have a lot of energy. She also said I would write books and I have a strong connection to supernatural beings.

If it had been a regular reading, she most likely would have gone on about a girlfriend and money, as most fakes do. I don't know if she was for real, but looking back just a few months later, I was inclined to think it was a legitimate reading.

Later, Shi-Ji also said I have a lot of energy, and that the key to understanding everything is to understand energy.

CHAPTER 18

ORB WITH A FACE

Nothing unusual happened for a couple of weeks after my first visit from Shi-Ji, but what she said was playing on my mind, and my life was changing.

The orbs (balls of light) around the house continued, and soon enough I had a weird encounter with one and caught it on camera.

On the 20th of January 2012, I woke up at about 7:00 a.m. in the morning. As soon as I opened my eyes, I saw an orb fly out of my bedroom and go to the lounge room; it was just zipping around doing whatever orbs do.

So I grabbed the camera next to my bed, turned it on, and took a photo. The orb continued flying around for about 30 seconds, coming in and out of view from where I was in my bed. I got up and went to see if it was still there, but it seemed to have disappeared.

So I went outside and had a look. Then I went back inside, made a coffee, and waited around to see if anything else would happen.

The orb emanated blue light and there appeared to be a burgundy color inside the light. I had never seen an orb like this one before, but it was enough to get my blood pumping for the day.

Questions played on my mind after this incident: *What was it, and what was it doing in my bedroom?* Maybe I'll never know, but it certainly was interesting.

Later the same day, when I put the photo of the orb on my computer, I realized it seemed to have a face.

I had not noticed the orb had a face while I was watching it fly around. Perhaps I was still sleepy or just in awe about it. All I know is that it was there; it flew out of my room as soon as I woke up; and it continued to fly around the lounge room until it disappeared.

Now...what are orbs? Personally, I believe there are many different types and many are the pure essence of a being when not in a body. I also believe some beings are always an orb. I also believe the color of an orb shows the level of its enlightenment and energy.

Orbs have been known to do surveillance on abductees, cause electrical interference, and burn objects. There is some evidence of this on video.

Also there is scientific evidence in the crop circles, where orbs have been seen and filmed on video at the site, during, before, and after the crop circles appear, and that when they check the makeup of the crop, the plants have been changed. I found this out while doing research into UFOs. Scientists say the effect on plants is caused by high energy.

Also there are nature orbs, and ones that look over beings; there are many different types.

Orbs are common in the paranormal field; they are connected to both haunted locations and UFO activity. Hauntings are different, but as I mention in Part One of this book, there are different types of hauntings.

One type of haunting is a "residual haunting," which is when you get the same activity over and over, like a tape recorder playing on repeat.

When this is reported and proven, I believe the energy from an event—or energy connected to a person who was once in the location—has been left behind as an "energetic imprint." This causes a residual haunting. Many people in the paranormal field agree with this theory.

The other type of haunting is an "intelligent haunting." This is where the spirit, ghost, or whatever you want to call it, can interact, move things around and so on.

I believe this happens when a spirit hangs out in a particular location because it has strong ties to the location, or to get a point across, or they aren't ready to move on yet, or they don't know how.

Also with an intelligent haunting you might be communicating with something in another dimension, or with someone or something at another point in time.

You might be dealing with elementals (nature spirits), otherworldly beings, or beings from other dimensions. So not all spirits or ghosts were once in human form. I believe the paranormal field and the E.T reality are connected.

Now...I don't claim to know everything, but this is just my take on orbs and what they might be. It's not like we can have a conversation with one, or can we?

CHAPTER 19

BLACK HELICOPTERS

Talk about coincidences. In Part One, I wrote about a black helicopter appearing over my house, after a blue orb visited me. Well…it happened again after the incident with the orb that had a face.

Some of the helicopters that have flown over my house have not just been unmarked black helicopters. They have also been dark green and a light grey color, and also unmarked.

The following incident occurred around 8:00 p.m. just before dark on the 21st of January 2012.

I was inside on the computer, when all of a sudden I heard a helicopter. It sounded like it was right over my house. Straight away I grabbed the camera and went outside, and there it was: a light grey unmarked helicopter. It was flying very low and it circled my place two times. Then it went southwest. I had never seen a helicopter like it before. It had a very smooth and stealthy look about it.

Many have said these types of helicopters monitor and intimidate contactees, abductees, and people in the UFO field. So this might be what has been happening to me. All I know is that they appear very low above my house and fly in circles. This is all I can really say. Also they have appeared before and after sightings of UFOs.

Now I am inclined to believe they are trying to catch my otherworldly visitors "in the act." I have come to this conclusion because I have come across this in other cases, and, as I said, the fact that they are flying over my place before and after UFOs appear over my house might not be a coincidence. It really seems like the only logical explanation.

The thing that gets me, though, is the fact they know when I'm being visited. The reason I say this is because *I don't even know when I'm going to be visited!*

Why do they do this, when I live in such a small city? Are they oblivious to the fact that they stand out? I think not. I just think they couldn't care less, because they have a job to do. This has occurred a few times.

As of late, two friends have talked to me about the helicopters. They have seen them on two separate occasions over the block where my house is located.

CHAPTER 20

SHI- JI FLIES BY

My suspicions about the purpose of the unmarked helicopters were confirmed when I had my next visit from Shi-Ji.

It was around 11:00 a.m. on the 22nd of January 2012, the day after the grey helicopter flew over. I was in my house relaxing in front of the television, when I started to get a cold feeling on my forehead. Then I heard Shi-Ji say, "Pete, it's me, Shi-Ji," in my mind.

I looked around my lounge room and she was nowhere to be seen, so I checked the rest of the house. Then I heard her say "Out the back, Pete, out the back."

So I went outside and there was a UFO just flying around. It was different from the other UFOs I had seen up to this point. Straight away I ran back into the house, grabbed my camera, and went back outside to take a photo.

Now…up to this point I had never seen a UFO like this. It was crazy. The only thing I can tell you about it is the bottom was as black as anything could be. It was so black! I have never seen a black darker than the bottom of that UFO. It's really hard to explain.

Also the top of the craft was metallic, but I could not make out the shape of the overall craft. It might have been a disc or a ball type craft, but I really couldn't tell because I was so occupied with thinking about how black the bottom of the craft was. The bottom did not seem to be a physical part of the ship. It was more like a black hole.

Straight after I took the picture, Shi-Ji told me telepathically to practice harnessing my feelings. This will open me up to seeing and being aware of what's really around me. She said I need to have patience and learn how to relax, and doing so will intensify my frequency.

Before I knew it, the UFO had disappeared, and that was that. I had been caught off guard and left wondering: *What was all that about? Why doesn't she fly closer to my house? Why didn't she pop in and say hello?*

Later I thought about how uncomfortable it is that she can speak directly into my mind anywhere, anytime, and how she can pop up anywhere, anytime. It was all so new and so much to take in.

The fact that I had been contacted face to face and telepathically by a being from another world was confusing, to say the least. I kept telling myself: *No, I'm not crazy; this is really happening.* But it was difficult to believe.

For years I had been searching for answers, and now I was finally getting them. So if this is part of the ride, it's part of the ride. I don't know how to put it any other way, except to say that seeing Shi-Ji and the light being were "out of this world experiences." It was much like seeing a ghost, except it had even more impact. It forced me to face the fact that there is more "out there" than I ever imagined. These meetings with Shi-Ji challenged every belief I had previously held.

CHAPTER 21

LIFE SEEMS MUNDANE

After the last visit from Shi-Ji, life started to seem mundane because now I understood earthly reality is not what it seems. Everything that had happened up to this point was a mystery, but I was getting answers and the process was fascinating. Nothing else mattered.

I had met and was getting to know a being from another planet. How incredible is that? UFOs are fascinating, but even the sightings started to seem like second nature after meeting Shi-Ji.

Don't get me wrong, seeing and witnessing UFOs is a life-changing and mind-opening experience, but I had already experienced many sightings, so UFOs were not so much of a mystery anymore. Also, I knew instinctively that more would be revealed, in time.

Questions! I had so many questions:

Where exactly in the Pleiades is she from?

What is the environment like on her planet?

And what about social structure and community?

Do they have different countries and how do they govern them?

Then I started to wonder about how far ahead of us they are:

Do they have wars like we have here on earth?

Her genetics came to mind. Shi-Ji looks completely human, except for how big her eyes are, her telepathic abilities, and being able to teleport. Was this natural for them, or did they come across this ability or develop it over time? What are the differences between their genes and ours?

I thought about the types of food they eat, if any at all, and if they had farms and animals like here on earth.

There was no limit to my questions, which threatened to overload my mind: *Do they have different races on her planet?*

Are they working with other races from different planets other than their own, located in other places in space, and if so, how does all that work?

She talked about other groups, but what exactly did she mean?

Were there laws, judges, and the like?

Do they get married?

Do they work at jobs?

Do they have homes, and how do they generate power for their crafts and homes.

What do they do for entertainment?

Have they ever communicated with our government or any other government on earth?

I wondered how many people Shi-Ji had actually communicated with who were average people like me. And "yes," I still had the question: *Why me? What's so special about me?*

I could go on and on….

Luckily, for my own sanity, some of these questions, and more, would be answered, in time, bringing peace and understanding and lifting much of the weight off my shoulders.

CHAPTER 22

THE LIGHT BEING POPS IN AGAIN

My next experience was on the 9th of February 2012.

I was at home in my lounge room and had just finished lunch at around 1:30 p.m. After going to the kitchen to clean up, I returned to my couch to lay back and let my body digest the food. Without warning, the Light Blue Light Being" showed up again.

It happened without notice, like the first time I saw it and just like Shi-Ji when she appears. As with the first incident, the Light Being appeared in the middle of my lounge room— its light blue light body making the room light up with white light.

As before, it seemed to stare at me, while emanating feelings of love, authority, wisdom, and knowledge.

Next I woke up on the computer in my office, which is my spare bedroom. Realizing where I was and that it was around 4:00 p.m., it sunk in that I again had "missing time."

I don't know what happened, only that I had two and a half hours of "missing time," and the last thing I saw was the Light Being in my lounge room. So…now I've had "missing time" twice.

Another bizarre event happened a week later.

It was the 16th of February 2012 around 11:00 p.m. at night. I had just finished watching television and was starting to get sleepy, so it was time for bed. I got up and walked to my bedroom, hopped in bed, and closed my eyes.

Before I knew it, I saw flashes of lightning that seemed to come from somewhere in my room— *even though my eyes were closed*. There was no storm or lightning outside and no one was in my house, so I thought it was a bit odd.

When I opened my eyes, I saw something so strange and incredible. I had never seen anything like it before, nor have I seen it since. I can only describe it as a "Sheet of White Light" that was see-through and about half the size of my queen-size bed. It was hovering over my body, about three feet above me in midair.

Before I knew it, this "thing" slowly moved out of my bedroom and went into my lounge room, and then disappeared.

I got up and looked around the house. Finding nothing to explain this apparition, I sat up for the rest of the night watching television and thinking about what had just happened. There was no way I could go back to sleep because I was so pumped from the experience.

The weird thing about the Sheet of Light was that even though it was white, the inside of it looked like the northern lights. For example, there was mainly a light green color swirling within the white light, and there were blue and purple colors in it, too. *It was one of the most beautiful things I had ever seen*.

What was it? I don't know, but it was an experience I will never forget. Words cannot adequately describe the Sheet of White Light and how beautiful it was.

CHAPTER 23

SHI-JI DROPS IN

A bit after mid-February 2012, I closed down "UFO Update Daily" and "IFTT" (Investigators For The Truth), where I took UFO reports and conducted investigations into the paranormal for free (which were also the websites I was running). All of these activities had become too much because of what was happening to me personally.

I needed to concentrate on my experiences, because since meeting Shi-Ji the action had not stopped. Also, I no longer needed the answers I had been seeking.

On the 27th of February 2012, Shi-Ji came to see me again. This time, she revealed more about why she had been visiting me.

It was morning and I had just gotten out of the shower, put on my clothes, and was combing my hair. The next thing I knew, Shi-Ji was talking in my head saying, "Pete, it's me, Shi-Ji. I'm in your lounge room."

So I walked out to the lounge room to meet her, and there she was, standing in the lounge room at the front door. This time she had her hair tied back and she was wearing light blue pants, a black top (that was not a turtleneck like the last time), and light blue shoes. All her garments appeared again to be made from material similar to that of a wetsuit.

I welcomed her as she walked to the middle of the lounge room, and we started to talk. The funny thing is that during this conversation, I was speaking verbally *and* telepathically, but I didn't realize it until she brought it up. Shi-Ji didn't seem to mind. She said it was good practice for me to communicate telepathically while she was around, and that either way was fine.

"I know you have many questions," she said. "And I would be happy to talk with you about them, but I can only answer what I am allowed to answer."

The first thing I said was, "Why do you fly your craft only so close?"

"We would get what you call "sick" if we came too close to the town, because of the difference in the energy between the people of earth and my people," she said, adding, "Getting any closer to show you the craft is not worth getting sick."

I told her I understood, and then proceeded to ask why her craft comes as close as it does, and why so many people have been seeing UFOs.

"Pete, your energy is good enough for us to be in direct contact. Also, in places where a lot of people have good energy, they can see us, too."

"How come the others on your craft can't come down and see me?"

"You only have so much energy, Pete," said Shi-Ji.

When I questioned her as to what she meant, she said getting closer to me doesn't make her feel sick because she is able to use my energy, but if the others did it at the same time, or even a few did, I would not be able to handle it and I would collapse from my energy being drained.

After taking in this information, I asked her, or rather tried to confirm her meaning. "So is it all about energy?"

"Correct," said Shi-Ji.

I asked her why she was visiting me and what she meant when she told me a month or so ago about my vibrational frequency and raising it, and also about my being awakened.

"You are very special, Pete, as are all humans. Your connection to Source is very strong because of your energy and frequency. You have a high frequency that can tap into any other frequency. You have only noticed this the last few years because more of the same energy has entered the earth dimension."

Shi-Ji added that, in the past, it was not noticeable to me because others around me did not have the same energy. "You were unaware because you didn't know how to tune into the lower frequency of the other humans around you," she said. "But you do now because you have been growing as a result of your soul-searching and research."

This brought up another question, so I asked her, "When you talked about Source, did you mean the God Source, The Creator, The One you spoke about when we first met?"

Shi-Ji replied by saying that I already knew the answer to this question, but then she said, "Yes," because she knew I needed confirmation for my peace of mind.

"You don't know who you really are, but through meditation, you will find out. You have tapped into another part of yourself in space and time, in another dimension, in an area located many light years away on the other side of the universe. Through meditation, more will be revealed to you."

Everything she was saying made sense. It almost seemed like I already knew the truth of it, but was only recognizing it now.

I asked her again about what she meant when she said, "You are being awakened."

"I am here with many others to help awaken those who are ready to wake up. You must help awaken other humans through your energy and by writing and telling your story. In time, you will understand."

Next she told me, "Just think about energy, bliss, and love, because this is your true nature. Over time, this practice will bring you back to being your true self."

It was difficult to take in so much information, but that wasn't all. I knew she had more to teach me.

Next...I asked her why the bottom of the last craft I'd seen (when she last spoke to me) was so black.

"I cannot say at this time because you are not ready for this information. But you will find out for yourself as you continue evolving through meditation."

I asked her why she had brought up religion.

"It's not so much the religions I'm encouraging you to think about," she said. "But the Masters, beings like Jesus and Ezekiel."

I asked her what she meant, and she said she knew I believed in the Creator, but I was not sure about religions and the prophets. She said this was logical on my part, because a lot of what the Masters teach has been misrepresented. I already knew what she meant and we were in complete agreement.

"In time, you will all become Masters. Humans are very special because you are a link between the Angels (which are enlightened beings), and Source. You are all God—you are all part of The One, The Creator."

She continued to explain that most of the people known throughout the earthly religions as God, or Gods, were actually extraterrestrial. They were real, but because they were more advanced than humans, and because they abused the power of being more advanced, things did not turn out as originally intended. This meant evolution had to be restarted here on earth, time and time again.

"You must not worship another, but realize that you are all part of the Creator. Each of you has a part of God within you. You *are* God."

"What does this mean for me?"

She said the information she was conveying was very important, and I would recognize this, in time, as I tap into all levels of consciousness.

"Worrying will not help, but being patient will show you the way."

After absorbing everything Shi-Ji had said, I asked if there were other groups of races or beings out in the universe that she or her people work with, because I wasn't sure what she meant when she talked previously about other groups.

"Yes. All of the universes are full of life, existing in forms you can hardly imagine," she said. "I work with some groups and the Council monitors it all."

I asked her what she meant by the "Council."

"Imagine the earth is the universe and then imagine each country as a galaxy, and then you have planets in each galaxy, but imagine them as states, cities, and towns. This is how the Council monitors everything: with Council Members representing each area. Each group communicates with one another in an organized fashion, and those are the others we work with. There are thousands of others."

"For the most part, this is how it works, although some groups are not a part of it. There are thousands of groups, and earth is on the brink of playing its part in the evolution of the universe."

I asked Shi-Ji if the UFOs I've been seeing are her crafts. "No," she said. "You have also been seeing crafts from other groups.

I asked her who they are, but she said she could not tell me because it was not her place to tell me, and that I would find out, in time.

Without warning, she put her hand on my forehead, which was very cold, and before I knew it, I was having visions and hearing voices in my head, as if I had just downloaded all this information. It was very draining. "I feel like I'm about to pass out," I told her.

Shi-Ji said that was enough for now and, before I knew it, she was gone. I lay down on the couch, closed my eyes, and went to sleep. She had relayed a lot information and I needed to rest and take it all in.

Looking back on this conversation with Shi-Ji, I find it interesting that Jesus in the New Testament talks to a crowd and tells them they are all God. He also says that he is not from "here," but from "up there."

CHAPTER 24

VISIONS

Over the next few days after seeing Shi-Ji, I pondered on what she had said and did a lot of relaxing and meditation. In other words, I had a time out. I wanted to get away from the world we think we know and just let everything she had said be absorbed into my human mind.

Around this time, I started to have actual visions while fully awake. This was very uncomfortable, at first. I would be doing whatever, when all of a sudden, I would see actual scenes or places, but I could still see where I actually was (in my body). It was like looking into two completely different places at the same time, because I could see where I was and the vision at the same time.

It was very annoying as it continued. At first, I didn't know what to think. Nothing like it had ever happened to me before, except for when I did remote viewing. It still continues up to this day, every now and then.

I saw events that were taking place all over the world. I could see whole cities destroyed and large numbers of bodies lying on the ground. I saw giant tsunamis, earthquakes wiping out whole cities, and the sky turning red, and more.

At first, it was very upsetting and put me in tears. *Why am I seeing such bad things?* I wondered. But, in time, the visions went from being negative to visions of love and beauty. I saw beautiful land and healthy people brimming with love and equality. Everything started to appear like there was peace on earth in a crystal clear way.

Around the 10th of March 2012, I had a mind-opening and soul-evolving experience. While meditating, I had a vision of a light world with two beings. They were standing close to me and looking straight into my eyes.

One was a man and the other was a lady. They appeared human, and behind them were many other beings, all dressed in white robes.

This place and these beings felt like home. I can't say anything more, because words can't describe how loving this place was and how loving the beings were.

The man was white and had grayish white hair and a beard, and he was wearing a white robe. He had blue eyes that looked into my eyes, and I got the feeling of so much love, like a father to a son. He also had a great big smile.

The lady also showed me so much love. It was like a wave that flowed out of her and enveloped me—I can't really describe it any other way. She had the reddest lips I have ever seen; her skin was white; and she was wearing a white robe with a hood. She had light brown hair with a tint of red in it. Her eyes were also blue, and she smiled at me like we were old friends.

Before I knew it, the vision stopped and I was back at home, confused but happy, and wondering what had just happened.

Soon I would find out who these beings were, and it ended up being a huge surprise.

Around this time I started to write about my awakening, as Shi-Ji and the psychic said I would. For some reason I just got this urge. I had to express my feelings about everything that was going on and get it out of my system.

Everything fell into place, because the company I worked for was bought by another company, and I was back to looking for work. So I had plenty of time to write.

CHAPTER 25

SHI-JI COMES CALLING

On the 14th of March 2012, Shi-Ji visited me again, and we had a conversation that really opened my mind because she offered more answers to my questions. I didn't even have to ask many of them, because she already understood much of what I wanted to know.

The weather was stormy and I felt drained because I had been editing one of my books and was mentally exhausted. So to recuperate, I went into the lounge room, did some mediation, and was out of it for about two hours.

Afterwards, I got up to make some tea, when all of a sudden, Shi-Ji called me out to the back. So I went outside, but no one was there.

Then I heard her say, "Concentrate and let everything go."

After about 40 seconds, I looked up and I could see her craft high in the sky, so I went back inside, grabbed the camera, and ran back out to take a photo. Then her craft disappeared.

Straight away Shi-Ji appeared next to me in the backyard, but I noticed something different about her.

She was wearing a black turtleneck top with light blue pants and black shoes. Her garments looked to be made of the same wetsuit material as before, and her hair was loose. *She also appeared to be see-through.* It was like looking at a ghostly image of her.

Then she disappeared.

Next I heard her say, "In here," so I went inside and there she was in my kitchen.

"How ya doing, Shi-Ji?"

"Hello, Pete."

"What happened just then?"

She replied by saying she wanted me to come out back and learn more about my ability to harness energy, because it was the only way I would be able to see her craft.

I was still wondering why she looked see-through when we were out back, so I asked her: "Why were you see-through just now? It made me a bit uncomfortable to see you that way."

"The rays of the sun and the energy outside sometimes make me appear see-through because I am from the fifth dimension. This can sometimes happen."

Then she said she called me inside so nobody would hear me talking with her and think I was talking to myself.

As she went on about higher frequencies and the fifth dimension, I felt my mind being altered and expanding in ways I never thought possible.

"People like you, Pete, who vibrate at a higher frequency, can see me as I am, a fifth dimensional being. It is also possible for other humans with a high frequency to see me, too. But the average person can only see me when I lower my frequency. I do this, on occasion, depending on the circumstances."

Shi-Ji went deeper and more expansive:

"You have also experienced the fifth dimension, Pete, and many other dimensions, many times. Seeing me in my fifth dimensional form might have shocked you, like a "flashback" from a time when you were doing what I do: visiting other dimensions and planets. You chose to forget this ability when you decided to take human birth.

I replied by saying that I was concerned and uncomfortable seeing her that way. She said I felt this way because I was in a human conscious mind.

"So right now someone could be here with me and not see you?"

"Correct, but that's not all," she continued. "Anyone with high energy will be able to notice me."

Then she giggled.

More and more questions were arising in my mind. "What you just said about my doing in the past, what you're doing now—what did you mean?"

Shi-Ji explained that in my past lifetimes, in other parts of the universe and in multiple dimensions, I was like her, but to a lesser extent. She said in the past I was an overseer.

At this point, I really didn't know what to think.

She said I would realize this, in time, because my subconscious and conscious mind are starting to act as one, and soon I would remember things from other lives in other places.

"You were not chosen to come here. You chose to be born on earth," said Shi-Ji.

I asked her what she meant, to which she replied, "You choose to come here for this very important time that earth is going through. You are meant to be here and do what you are doing, because you are a worker of light, a worker of energy.

This information was very hard for my conscious mind to take in.

Shi-Ji explained she thought I would have realized this by now, because I have been visiting places during meditation that are not accessible by the average human being.

She said she recently received a message from her Elders about me being in contact with beings in one of the places I visited. They told her that I am able to do more in this body than they expected.

Shi-Ji also told me that I had visited the dimension of Christ Consciousness.

Now it gets even more trippy!

"It's the place of light you visited recently," she said.

"Do you mean the place where I saw the man and a lady in white robes with other beings behind them?"

"Yes," she said. "That's correct."

All of a sudden I started to feel sick from a rush of adrenalin, almost a sense of panic. *How does she know all this stuff about me?*

"It's okay, Pete, you're just a bit shocked by what I'm telling your conscious mind."

"Too right," I said.

"The place you visited can be accessed anytime through what you're doing [meditation]."

"Well… who are the beings I saw?"

"You already know the answer to that question, Pete."

"Not really," I said.

She went on to say that after this incident she was aware I had searched everywhere to try and find a statue of the lady I'd seen, and nothing matched it because there is nothing that matches it.

She was correct, too. When thinking about this experience later, I remembered thinking I had seen the lady before somewhere, as a statue or in a religious picture.

I was still curious about the lady. "Who is she?"

"It was Mary," said Shi-Ji. "And the man you saw was Moses."

This seemed so strange that I started to think she was joking.

She went on to say that I need to stop being stubborn about the things I know, and to stop blocking my subconscious, which defeats all the hard work I'm doing.

Shi-Ji told me to go with my "gut instinct," to trust it. She said to stop ignoring my feelings. She reinforced the idea that I am not imagining the unusual events and experiences occurring in my life.

"I can see you are drained. It's been a big day and you have enough to think about."

So I thanked her for visiting and said I would see her later.

She smiled, had a bit of a giggle, and disappeared.

After this incident, I started to think about her being an inter-dimensional being and how the crafts I have been seeing are also inter-dimensional.

I thought about how big things are in the universe, or as she said, "the universes."

It made me think about how there is so much more intelligent life out there in places we can't even imagine, and how the needs of these otherworldly beings and their way of life are totally different from ours.

I also realized how lucky I am to have these experiences. I should be grateful and not ask stupid questions like I had planned—about what they eat and how they live—because beings in different dimensions might not have the same needs we do, living in a human body, and the human race really won't be able to comprehend it until full disclosure and enlightenment.

This put things into more of a perspective, because it was a blessing to be visited by Shi-Ji. But like she said, "You're not the only one I'm visiting and waking up here on earth."

This also explains why her visits are so short. There must be a lot for her and her group to do—and because I only have so much energy.

Shi-Ji's comments that I used to do what she does, and meeting Moses and Mary, were a lot to take in. I still have a hard time believing it.

CHAPTER 26

THINKING ABOUT THE PAST

Shi-Ji had said so much during her last visit. All her talk about dimensions, energy, my other lives, and my choosing to come to earth was a lot to take in.

The information she shared fit in with my beliefs about reincarnation and with living many lives and growing and learning until we become Masters, and with ascending as we evolve until we reach a point of high knowledge, and then we go back to the God Source—which we all came from. But having it all laid out for me, and also the fact that it came from Shi-Ji, an inter-dimensional being, was overwhelming.

It played on my mind because all of it seemed believable, rather than unbelievable. A lot of what she said didn't really surprise me. It was like I already knew it, but my mind couldn't handle the conscious overload.

I had to pull myself back and look at things differently. Then I thought: *The next time I see her, I really want to focus on a few things from before meeting her, and about who I was before entering this life.*

I also wanted to know more about the orbs I had seen. I believed that when more of my questions were answered, it would be easier to embrace my purpose, my "job." I would be able to understand the events of my life and start working everything out for myself. Basically, I would be able to see the bigger picture. The more I thought about it, the more questions arose:

Who is the blue guy I see during remote viewing when meditating?

Why did it take so long for her to visit me, and why now?

What happened when I had "missing time"?

Who or what is the Light Being?

What did she mean about me coming from a higher dimension in my past lives?

Why did I choose to come here? And why now?

Over the next few days, I started to realize I had a mission on earth and it was time to get serious. This made me think about timing. Maybe I met Shi-Ji when I did because that's how it was meant to be. I had to be ready for our meeting.

* * *

From about fourteen years of age until twenty-three, I was very impatient. As a teen, I was "off the rails," and if I were Shi-Ji, I wouldn't have come near me, either! I was arrogant and thought the world revolved around me. Being a well-known rap artist made me think: *This is my life. This is how it's meant to be.*

I had many friends (good and bad), and experimented with drugs, which I'm not proud of. I don't regret the past because it helped me evolve into the man I am now. I just look back and feel disappointed with my behavior. I never violently hurt anybody, because it was not in my heart, but I wasn't real with myself, or the people around me. This showed up in my music, because a lot of the stuff I wrote about was negative, though a lot of it had a positive message. I know now that person wasn't truly me. The people around me told me what I wanted to hear, not what they really wanted to say.

Eventually I cleaned myself up and went back to studying and looking after my body. Around that time, everything from UFOs to orbs started popping up again, as I wrote about in Part One.

Soon I found out the negative aspects of my early life had played an important part in my development, in terms of being able to astral travel and to clear my mind through meditation.

I still wonder why I chose to come to earth and live as I did when I was younger. But now I believe my conscious mind won't understand it all until I become more enlightened.

The only way to attain enlightenment is to experience all the good and bad, and learn from it. I think I'm doing that.

CHAPTER 27

SHI-JI TELLS ALL

Soon enough Shi-Ji popped in again and offered insight into my role, and why so many strange things have been happening. On the 19th of March 2012, around midday, she appeared in my office at home. I was working on the computer, when all of a sudden I heard her say, "Hello Pete."

A little shocked, I turned and there she was, standing in the middle of the room. "Hey Shi-Ji" I said, and straight away I asked her about the Light Being that appears in my house sometimes.

"The Light Being you see is highly evolved compared to me, and also to you. In time, you will get the answer to your question. This is all I'm allowed to say right now."

I asked her if she knew why I had "missing time" after the last time I saw the Light Blue Light Being, and what happened when I had "missing time" last year after seeing the red orb.

"These events have to do with monitoring your energy, altering your DNA, and energizing your body so you can better handle The Shift," she said."

Then she added she could say nothing more about it, and that, in time, I would learn more about the Light Being and the red orb. "Many types of beings are at work here; some are watchers, some are protectors, and some are doing the work for the coming Shift."

This was all she would say on the matter.

I didn't press her any further, because I understood that if she couldn't tell me, she couldn't tell me. It didn't bother me, because I had a few more questions. So I asked her to tell me more about the orbs.

"You already know the answer to this question, Pete. Yes…they are beings in pure form at different levels of knowing and enlightenment. They are all individuals, there are many types, and all are connected."

Her expression indicated I could have asked a better question.

I asked if she knew anything about the blue guy I see when remote viewing during meditation.

"He is an advanced being who lives in the realm of universal consciousness. He monitors what you are doing, and also what many others are doing. There are many of his kind. You should have known by now not to be afraid of him."

I agreed with her, and said I did know about him, but I needed it confirmed for my own peace of mind.

Before I could ask another question, she said she already knew what I was going to say: "Why have I had so many sightings of UFOs and orbs, and what is the connection to being awakened?"

She was correct; this was exactly what I wanted to know.

"You need to be awakened slowly, gradually, and in a way that will cause minimal shock, because you are still in a conscious mind. If your awakening had occurred earlier, it might have been harmful because you were not ready."

She spoke about how I would eventually realize my true nature on my own by studying spirituality and meditating. She said my questions and the way I handled my unusual experiences showed this to be true, even as I was still immersed in the ways of the world.

Shi-Ji then went on to say this was confirmed when I was nineteen years old and contacted the "higher me." At first, I didn't know what she was going on about. But then she talked about when I was on top of a mountain during a storm.

This absolutely freaked me out, because only a few people knew of this experience.

She said that when this happened, I had broken the first barrier to finding out "who I am" and "my purpose in life." She was referring to an event that occurred when I was about nineteen years old and stupid—I took some "Tripstasy."

Tripstasy is a mixture of LSD and ecstasy in tablet form. I was told to take half of one tablet because it was really strong. But it was too late. As soon as my mate gave it to me, I swallowed it whole.

Straight away they said, "That's not good."

One of my mates drove a couple of my friends in his car and followed me as I drove my car back to my house. As soon as I arrived home every single light source was a flame. Next I went inside and sat on the couch.

I started to lose it and have visions. I told everyone they had to leave. Before I knew it, I was closing my eyes on the couch and hoping the visions would stop. But they wouldn't.

Soon I was able to close my eyes and relax, but when I opened them, *I was on top of a mountain.* It was so beautiful. I was an old man sitting with my legs crossed, wearing a blue and white robe, and I had white hair and a white beard.

I felt like I knew everything and was one with all.

The sky was purple, there were gray storm clouds, and it was lightly raining. The rain was just perfect, and there were flashes of lightning and the sound of thunder.

Looking down from the mountain, I saw a lush, green landscape with beautiful plants and trees.

There were flowers everywhere. It was so beautiful.

I was just going in and out of meditation the whole time, and it seemed like that was all the being (who was me) did all the time: meditate. It was total bliss.

After coming out of it, I was back on my couch in my body at home.

For the following two days, I didn't get out of bed and thought about going to hospital. I felt like I was knocking on death's door. But just when I got to the breaking point, I felt my whole body spontaneously heal and that was that.

That same day, I tried to work out how long I had been in a state of meditation and concluded it was a bit over eleven hours, because I had swallowed the pill at 8:00 p.m. and my flat mate came home the next day around 8:00 a.m., which was around the same time I came out of it.

Now, so long afterwards, Shi-Ji was referring to the experience I had when I was nineteen.

"You had a near-death experience and the "higher you" had to swap bodies with the earthly you. Otherwise, you would have died. This experience shows you are able to handle more than expected."

She also told me I don't need drugs to leave the body, even though some people do it that way. It can be done naturally without taking drugs. I have heard of Shamans using drugs to tap into the spirit world and communicate with otherworldly beings, and that it's possible because some drugs affect the brain and allow us to see other realities.

It seems like this is what happened to me. I don't plan on using drugs or recommend using drugs to communicate with the spirit world.

Shi-Ji spoke again: "You were very negative at that time. Does that explain some things?"

I was too stunned to really say anything, but I replied "Yeah." This was totally unexpected. Now I knew what she meant when she said I don't know "who I really am."

How did Shi-Ji know about something that happened so many years ago?

"Once you have perfected patience, you will be able to join with your "other me" anytime," she said. "I understand it's annoying sometimes to be in the body, but that's because you haven't spent much time on this earth."

She also said this is why the doctors told me I suffer from anxiety and high blood pressure, and also why my ears keep ringing.

She said these symptoms would continue until The Shift is completed. She explained the reason I am in such a rush all the time is because I'm in a human body and everything seems so slow, like walking, talking, cleaning, or whatever. At the spirit level, I'm not used to being physical because I am not from here.

Now I understand why I have always felt out-of-place.

Next I said, "Hey, do you know what my visions mean? They started after the last time I saw you."

"Pete, you had visions of events that have happened or that are going to happened soon on earth. Even though some of your visions were upsetting, it's good you had them, because it means you are getting more in tune with the consciousness of the universe."

"Some of what you saw, Pete, were earth changes and the results of The Shift—which has already started. You also saw the end result. The north and south poles are moving, and your sun is going to throw out huge solar flares. This is part of The Shift. The earth changes and spiritual changes are one and the same. Soon you will be able to control what you see; you are just at the beginning of your development."

It was a lot to take in.

My next question was: "What do you mean about all the Masters of each religion being connected?" I wanted to confirm what she had said in the past.

"Nearly all religions have misinterpreted and misunderstood the teachings of the Masters, but there is no need for formal religion because we are all one," she said.

This was reassuring, because I was in the same frame of mind about religion. The Christian, Muslim, Hindu, and many other religions are talking about the same thing: The God Source, The Creator, The One.

My understanding of what Shi-Ji said about religions and the Masters is that we should not worship anything or anyone, but learn from what the Masters have to say. They are talking about the same "God Source" we are all part of.

Later, looking back on this, I think this is what Jesus meant when he said the Holy Spirit lives in all of us.

Shi-Ji said Jesus, Muhammad, Ezekiel, Mary, Moses, and many others knew this, and they have been trying to teach us that God is within us, but this understanding has been withheld from the people on this planet because of greed. This was not the original plan for us here on earth.

"Some of the genuine teachings are still in existence," said Shi-Ji. She also said, "The idea of Hell is made-up, fiction. But if humans don't live positively when they are incarnated in a body, they will have to come back and try again to learn their lessons, whether on the same planet or elsewhere."

She continued, saying, "It's actually more complicated. Most of the beings here on earth have come back many times, except for a growing majority like you, Pete, who are here to balance the energy until the end of The Shift. You and others like you are here to help, as the Masters do, when the time is right."

Shi-Ji went on to explain we are all a part of God, The One, The God Source, and the way religions go on about God is not truth. The Gods worshipped within religions are exactly the same as us— the only difference is they evolved higher a lot sooner than we did.

And they were extraterrestrials.

"In the past, extraterrestrials and extraterrestrial groups came to earth and announced they were

God, or Gods," said Shi-Ji. "But it was all for their own gain. God, The One, is not a man or a woman, or a being. It is the source of all things throughout the universe. Every being that exists is a cell of the Body of God—imagine a tiny bit of the God Source split up into zillions of spirits, all separate but still part of the whole."

She said everything Jesus did, including miracles, can also be done by us, once we have evolved sufficiently. Jesus said he was the Son of God, The One, but he also said we are all children of God. We are the sons and daughters of the real God, the Creator, The One, The God Source—the one we all come from and will return to.

"Some beings are more evolved than Jesus, and there are also beings even more evolved, and so it goes on and on," she said. With this statement, I felt my mind being stretched further and further. There seemed to be no end to the knowledge possessed by Shi-Ji.

She spoke about how we leave the God Source as individual beings in order to grow and evolve at different rates over billions of lifetimes. It doesn't just happened overnight. We go from simply existing, to experiencing every life form, from plants and animals, to humanoids, to light beings, to beings in many different dimensions. We experience everything. Then we go back to the God Source.

Shi-Ji then talked about how I am starting to tap into higher levels of consciousness, while still in this body. She said the events in my past, both planned and unplanned, have also helped me evolve more rapidly in the earth environment, in spite of a few setbacks.

Shi-Ji then said something I've been told before.

"When you are in a room, Pete, you can make people feel you without seeing you. This is done by thought. Just by thinking, you can change your reality, because everything is energy, thought, and sound."

"Having this ability and using it is your job on earth at this time. You must use these gifts to spread love, which will awaken people to their true nature. This is not done by preaching, but by thinking. When done through thought, people will be awakened. It's using the energy. "Think energy," she said.

She told me I am an activator, one of many assigned to facilitate change during The Shift. Shi-Ji also said we are all beacons of light, and that light is energy.

When The Shift is complete, some will stay and some will go to the "New World." I asked what she meant about the New World, and she said, "It's a place where those who raise their vibrational frequency will go."

I didn't understand this, but she said I would soon.

At this point, I told her I was starting to feel drained.

She seemed proud of me for acknowledging my feelings, because usually *she* tells me I'm drained. She uses my energy to manifest and always seems to know when it's time for her to leave. This is the only way we can chat face to face, because if she didn't use my energy she would feel sick.

It seems this is part of the plan—for Shi-Ji to find me (and others) by tracking my energy and awakening me.

Shi-Ji is my awakener and I am the awakener of others. It is now evident that this is my purpose, my "job."

Next...Shi-Ji disappeared.

I still didn't know what the light being was. But I had more answers to my questions than before, including answers to questions I didn't even know I had.

So it seems the "paranormal is really normal," it's just that we don't understand it yet. Shi-Ji had certainly provided me with a lot of "food for thought!"

CHAPTER 28

GOODBYE AND HELLO

So…there were questions Shi-Ji could answer, and some she couldn't. Looking back, and even now, I am grateful for her guidance and what has come of it.

I'm also grateful for the fact that I have been visited and not abducted.

Throughout my research I was, and still am, broken-hearted by how abductees and their families are affected and how, when trying to get help, there is no one to turn to. It hurts to know so many people think they're crazy.

I'm glad I didn't have to go through that, even though I still have to put up with many people thinking I'm crazy. Knowing what I know now, I have to laugh about it or else I would be crying.

But moving on…things were about to take a turn and get even crazier.

On the 28th of March 2012, around 6:00 p.m., I received another telepathic message from Shi-Ji. I was again at home, but this time I was cooking dinner.

She started communicating immediately, saying it was time for her to move on and continue her assignment of awakening others. She said she was pleased with how far I've come in a short amount of time, and I should continue meditating and evolving, and helping others on earth.

"You will be guided from now on by other beings. Soon you will find out who they are, along with some you already are acquainted with.

In my mind I said, "Thank you Shi-Ji," to which she replied, "It's time for you to do what you came here to do. Know we will meet again."

I felt a bit sad after hearing this, but I also realized I had to get on with my mission. So it was goodbye to Shi-Ji, and hello to whatever was going to happen next. Still, I wondered:

Who are the other beings she talked about, including the ones I already know?

When will I meet Shi-Ji again?

When she was speaking about other beings, was she speaking about the orbs or the Light Being I've already seen?

So the beautiful fifth dimensional being from the Pleiades was my awakener, and now it was up to me to play my part in the awakening of all on earth.

Humanity will evolve if we all do our part, whether it's through spreading love or opening the minds of everyone we come in contact with. As Shi-Ji said, "It can be done by projecting thoughts of enlightenment and by treating others as you want to be treated."

The information she offered about my higher self—by which I mean there is more than one of me and I am part of my higher self, located somewhere else in space and time—is something I hadn't heard of before. The easiest way for me to understand this is that my spirit split up, and it can be in different places and occupy different bodies at the same time.

If the God Source can do it, why can't we—once we reach a high point of enlightenment? After all, we are part of the God Source. We are all one and the same.

Although this idea was mind-opening to contemplate, Shi-Ji's comments about energy were hard to absorb. She told me to use my mind. Well...I can meditate, remote view, and astral travel, and it all starts with a thought, so why not?

I accept the idea that I came here with many others to help balance out the energy for The Shift, because I have been having experiences for a long time, and because something in me just knows it's true, even though I don't remember choosing to incarnate on earth.

Well... I best not ponder on it too much, because, either way, I accept the fact that I contain the energy and I'm here for The Shift. What will happen when The Shift is complete? I don't know, but it's already in progress. What I do know is that if all these extraterrestrials and beings are here and they are watching us, something important is going to happen.

For some, it's about raising their vibrational frequency, but slowly, so there's no shock. Think of it as having a pot filled with water on a hot stove and slowly warming it. It has to be done slowly.

As of late, Russian scientists have actually proven through testing that you can change DNA through frequency. Even as I write this, I am hearing a high pitch frequency that sometimes lasts for hours. This has been happening for a while. Other people tell me they have similar experiences.

I now believe that some of the people on the earth (like myself) have incarnated as humans to influence the events surrounding The Shift. Some people have said that aliens are not allowed to directly interfere with other civilizations unless the Council approves it. What better way to help than to become a part of the planet and be an active citizen?

Everything I have learned from Shi-Ji and my other unusual experiences is a fascinating mystery to be pondered, especially the idea that everything in the universe is interconnected: the

Masters, God, angels, ghosts, UFOs, and science. It's all one and the same. Even though science doesn't understand this concept yet, I believe one day it will—when more of us are enlightened.

Looking back and thinking about Shi-Ji, and how she is a fifth dimensional being, I realized she might not really look the way she appeared to me. Perhaps she only showed herself to me as a beautiful, female human being.

Her needs are different than the life forms in the third dimension. I believe fifth dimensional beings can appear in many forms, but not as a human in their natural form. Maybe they appear as Light Beings, like the one I have been talking about, or something similar.

I might be right. I might be wrong.

Shi-Ji said I have the answers and I will know more, in time. I believe some of what I have written about here explains some of the unexplained.

CHAPTER 29

FLICKERS OF LIGHT IN THE HOUSE

The 8th of April 2012 was Easter Sunday, and weird things happened around the house.

First of all, I noticed something had been moved. The reason I noticed this is because I'm a very tidy person and I have a place for everything. So unless I'm using something, it's in its proper place.

My morning routine was the same as always. I got up in the morning, walked into the office (which is my spare bedroom), turned on the computer, walked out to the lounge room, turned on the television, and then I made a coffee.

After I went back into the office, planning to get on the Internet. Straight away I noticed that a box containing the "Indiana Jones Crystal Skull Model" and the DVD that came with it had been moved. Now it was sitting in front of my computer monitor, which is not its usual location.

*Well...*I thought. *This is odd*, so I put it back in its usual place, on another desk in my office.

Later in the day, I started to notice flashes of light in the house every now and then. This happened a few times a minute over about 5 minutes. Then it would stop and start again randomly during the rest of the day.

During most of the day, I meditated on and off and listened to the radio, just relaxing. I didn't realize until later that the light flashes might have something to do with the skull and DVD being moved.

Later that night, the flashes started getting more and more intense, and I decided to get the camera and take a few pictures. So that's what I did. The camera caught an image of an orb, which I hadn't seen visually. It looked like a blue orb with the shape of a face in it, similar to the Light Blue Light Being I wrote about earlier.

After putting the photo up on the computer and looking at it, the hairs on the back of neck stood up! And my thoughts turned to what I'm telling you now, which is that the orb I took a photo of is the Light Blue Light Being before it fully manifests. The reason I think it might be the same being is because it's the same color: blue. Also the faces are very similar and have the same facial features. I got a photo of it just by luck, after seeing flashes of light around the house.

So if you can imagine a human form in light blue light form, and all its features being one and the same color, this is what it looks like. Also, it has white light coming from it.

Blue Orb Captured by Peter Maxwell Slattery

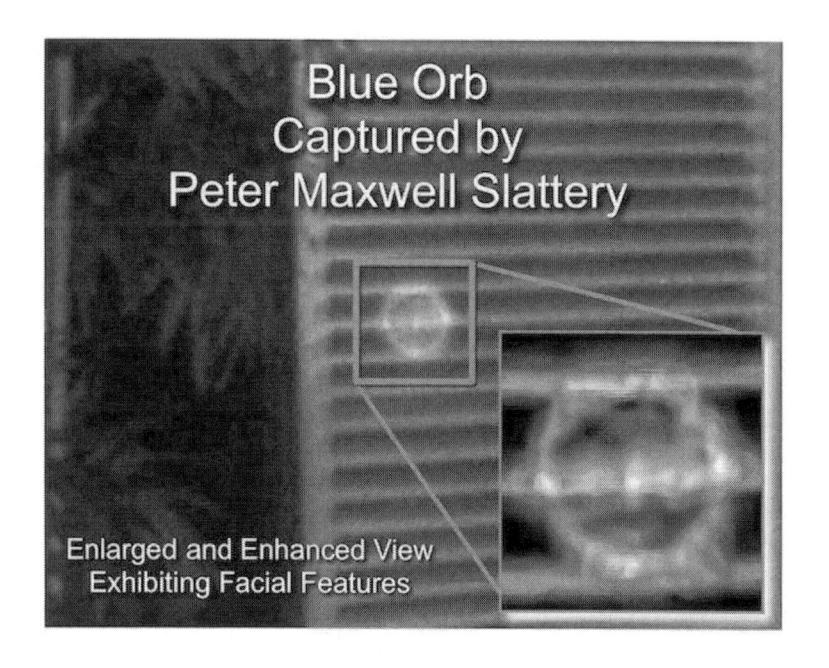

Enlarged and Enhanced View Exhibiting Facial Features

This is a photo of the blue orb with the face that was taken on the 8th of April 2012 analyzed by Jason Gleaves.

CHAPTER 30

CONFIRMATION

Something unexpected happened on the 17th of April 2012 in the afternoon. I received a phone call from a man who didn't know me. He said he just picked up his phone and dialed the number that was in his head, and I answered. He believed he was supposed to speak with me because I was the person who answered.

He said he was from northern New South Wales and he had a few questions for me.

Now…it wasn't unusual for me to get phone calls about UFO sightings, because I took reports for a while and got calls about paranormal activity. I've spoken with a Major, who was in the Army, and other people from all walks of life about their experiences, but this was different.

The guy was very intelligent, straightforward, and neutral in the way he spoke. He asked me if a UFO could single out a person and communicate by thought.

First, I asked him if he had seen a UFO. I also asked him what happened, what the craft looked like, the time, and so forth.

"Last night I woke up at 2:00 a.m. in the morning for no reason and walked outside," he said. "And there it was, a white light hovering in the sky about as high up as an aircraft would fly. It started to pulsate when I concentrated on it, and then it shot off. It was definitely not of this world."

I realized he was legitimate because of the way he answered my question.

He asked again, "Do you think they can communicate by thought?"

"It's possible," I said. "Some people who have reported a UFO sighting believe the beings on the craft know what they are thinking. The beings indicate this by moving the craft or making it pulsate. This has been reported all over the world many times."

Then the conversation took a turn. He said I am not insane, and that everything I'm experiencing is real.

Well...I was in shock and didn't know what to think.

I had his number on the phone and thought: *Well if it's a prank, I've got his number.* Then he asked for my name, which I was hesitant to give, at first, but I told him anyway. This was about ten minutes into the conversation.

By that time, it sounded like a different voice was coming through the phone every now and then.

Unexpectedly, the conversation changed totally, and I had the feeling he already knew the answer to the question he had first asked me (about whether a UFO could communicate with him telepathically).

He told me he has been having strange experiences all his life, and that for some reason he was meant to speak to me because my phone number came to him and he had an urge to pick up the phone—and because I answered.

The man was in his mid-sixties and seemed very together, but there was something unusual about him. He said he doesn't know me, and that he has been having weird experiences his whole life. He told me about a few that sounded very similar to mine. He said he believed Jesus and many others were Masters.

Shi-Ji had told me this, but the man called before I had time to tell anyone about what she said publicly. After that we talked on the phone about our experiences for an hour.

Mostly, I was just listening, but the whole conversation was really weird, because, somehow, it confirmed my own experience. Yes, Shi-Ji had given me confirmation, but it was good to hear it from another human being. Whoever he was, he knew a lot about me and he said didn't use the Internet.

Next...he started to say things about me that *nobody* knows, private things that only people close to me could know.

This was when I knew for sure something strange was going on.

He talked a lot about out-of-body traveling but didn't call it that. And he didn't know any of the terms I would use such as astral traveling or remote viewing, although this is what he was talking about. He also spoke about conversations he has had with otherworldly beings.

He kept saying, "You're not insane" and "All this is real."

The man spoke of human frequencies being raised and how some of us are going to raise our frequencies and go into the New World, and those who aren't ready will stay. Just like Shi-Ji had told me.

I asked myself: *How did we get on to talking about all this?*

Towards the end of the conversation, he started telling me about things in my house, where objects were, how I was living, and to keep doing what I'm doing, and to look after myself.

He even knew what dishes I had in the sink and where I was sitting!

I started to look around, while still talking on my mobile, to see if he was actually in my house and playing a prank.

Then he said he was sorry and he was going, because of the energy rush I was experiencing from his call. Before he hung up, he said if I ever needed to talk to someone I could call him. He also said I might not speak to him again, but that if I wanted to, I could.

Then he gave me his name, which I will not release.

Was he for real or not? I don't know, but this guy knew stuff about me no one else knows.

Later I started to wonder: *Is he one of the people Shi-Ji spoke about when she said I would start coming across others like me?*

CHAPTER 31

BLUEY

Now…just when I thought this book was finished a few more things happened.

On the 17th of May 2012, exactly a month after the phone call I wrote about in the last chapter, the Light Blue Light Being came for another visit.

I was on the couch in my lounge room, about to fall asleep while listening to the radio at around 11:00 p.m., when all of a sudden, I again saw what seemed to be flashes of lightning. I could see them with my eyes closed. When I opened my eyes, the Light Blue Light Being appeared.

Also, like the other times, it said and did nothing. It just stood there in the middle of my lounge room for about forty seconds and then disappeared.

After that, I was awake until the early hours of the morning thinking about it. I wondered how I could see the flashes of lightning when my eyes were closed, and how it seemed to be in the room with me. It was just like when the Sheet of White Light appeared with green, blue, and purple lights inside it. *Were these beings connected, the same being, or what?*

On the 1st of June 2012, something else happened.

I was sitting on the couch surfing the net on my laptop, when all of a sudden I saw a bright white light open up on my lounge room wall (to the right of where I was sitting).

A blue orb emerged from it.

The only way I can describe this is that it seemed like a portal from another dimension had opened up, and the blue orb came through it and into my lounge room.

Now…this thing was the same color blue as the Light Blue Light Being, which I assume is the light blue orb before it manifests into humanoid form. It was a bit bigger than the size of a golf ball.

The blue orb basically came out of the white light and went around my house like it was looking for something or inspecting my place. It went from the white light to the television, along the wall, past the heater, and then it went in to my spare room.

I was frozen with astonishment.

When I came back to the reality of what was happening, I got up and the blue orb went into my bedroom. Next, I went to the kitchen (which is right behind my couch) and grabbed the camera and turned it on.

Fortunately, this was good timing, because when the camera was ready to go, the blue orb came back into the lounge room and I was able to take a picture of it.

Straight after I took the picture, the orb went over the couch, where I was sitting, and went through the wall, exactly where the white light had appeared.

I went outside to see if I could find it.

What an experience!

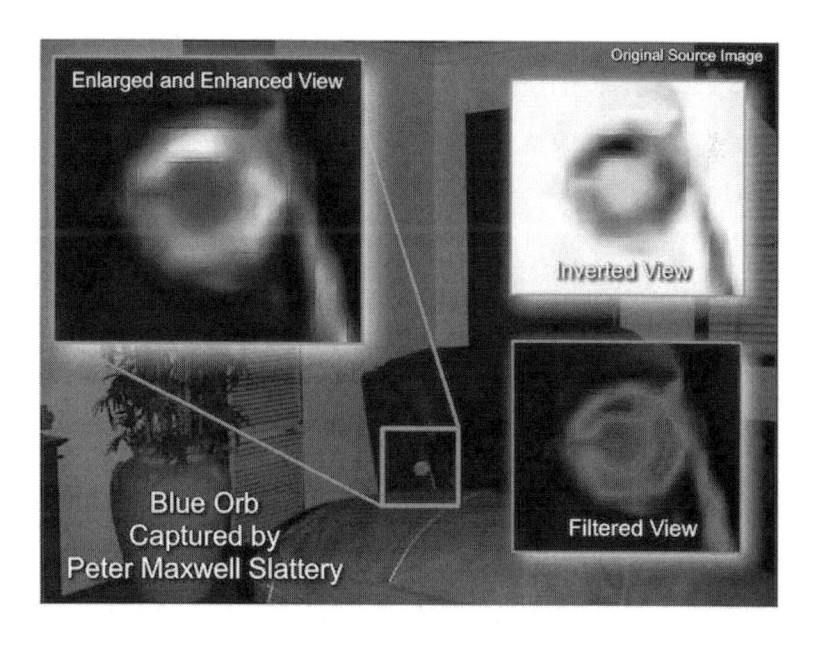

The 1st of June 2012 photo of the blue orb analyzed by Jason Gleaves.

CHAPTER 32

UNEXPECTED MESSAGE

Around this time, life was getting pretty full on. My first two books were out, I was on *Sunrise*, a Channel 7 morning news show here in Australia, and I was getting emails from people around the world.

All this I didn't mind because my story was getting around, but what I liked even more was that it was opening people up to the idea of the E.T reality, which is another reason why I'm coming out with my story.

Now…just when I thought things were getting quiet, I received another message from Shi-Ji.

It was the 3rd of July 2012, and I was answering emails in my office, when I decided to have a break and go to the kitchen for something to drink. When I got to the office door, Shi-Ji's voice sounded in my head, as she began talking to me telepathically.

This was totally unexpected.

"Ethereal, in the Pleiades," she said. Simultaneously, I saw a picture in my head of The Pleiades.

Then she said, "The fourth big star from the left." To which I replied, "Which one," because there were so many of them.

Next the vision in my head, zoomed in on that specific star and I heard Shi-Ji say, "Here, Pete, I'm from here."

Now...as I said, this was a telepathic message, but it was so clear—clearer than a person speaking out loud.

"This is only the beginning," said Shi-Ji, and I wondered what she meant.

What I do know, now, is what she means by "ethereal." Upon doing some research in the dictionary, I found out "ethereal" means, "light, airy, highly delicate, and heavenly." I also found a few pictures that are similar to what I saw in my head.

I believe the star Shi-Ji zoomed in on is called "Merope."

Now… As humans, we reside in the third dimension, the world of physicality. We could not survive in a fifth dimensional world, but Shi-Ji is an ethereal being, "light, airy, highly delicate, and heavenly" and she can.

So she is an ethereal being, living in an ethereal realm.

This opened up my mind even more.

The question of where Shi-Ji comes from had been playing on my mind since we first meet, but now I had an answer.

CHAPTER 33

REVELATIONS AND WHERE TO GO FROM HERE

So what's going to happen next? I don't know for sure.

What I do know is that after being visited by Shi-Ji and having UFO sightings since 1995 (which continue up to this day), is that anything is possible and anything can happen anytime.

Still...I get emotional at times with it all, even when writing my books. But it had to be done, because my story—when put together with other stories of being visited by otherworldly beings—is the most important story ever for humanity.

For now, it's time to play my part in the awakening of humanity through meditating, projecting (by thought) love to all on earth and out into the universes, and by educating those who are interested.

The process of awakening is quickening at this time, affecting all life on earth. It's my role, along with many others, to support all of humanity as we evolve during The Shift. As Shi-Ji said, "Keep doing what you're doing." So that is exactly what I'll do.

I already knew a lot of what Shi-Ji had to say, except for my role, which I now know is to increase awareness of the E.T. reality, and to help humans evolve as we move collectively through to completion of The Shift.

It's all up to us as to how humanity will evolve, individually and as a civilization. Some of us will stay on earth and others will go. I believe both physical and metaphysical change is going to occur on a large scale. The vibrational frequency of some will be raised, and many will be awakened.

The Shift won't necessarily be easy. We have some tough times ahead, and it is up to us individually and as a whole, how we deal with the coming spiritual and earth changes.

Now I understand what Shi-Ji meant about the New World, and she was right, now I do understand. It will be like it says in the Bible: two people will be in the field and one will go and one will stay; two people will be in bed and one will go and one will stay.

To me, this means those who increase their vibrational frequency will move into another dimension and go to the New Earth. Those who are not ready will stay on earth. It's all about energy. So when will these events happen? Who knows, but just like the Bible also says, when Judgment Day comes, it will be like a thief in the night.

The "judgment" will not be about who is going to heaven or hell. It will be about who is ready to go to the New Earth, and who is not. Those who are ready will go because their vibrational frequency has risen. I find it interesting that in the Book of Revelation in the Bible it also talks about a New World.

It's all part of The Shift, which has already started, and the New World, which already exists.

We are not alone and we are more than we know. We are special.

The time has come for the world to learn about the E.T reality and the multitude of beautiful beings and places in the universe. Soon it will also be time for the human race to play its part in the evolution of the universe.

It's also time for the awakener to awaken others, and a time of enlightenment for those who are ready to embrace it.

Peace, love, light, and bliss to all.

Pete Slattery

Books by Peter Maxwell Slattery

The Book of Shi-Ji

The Book of Shi-Ji 2

The Book of Shi-Ji 3

Connect to Your Spirit and ET Guides

About the Author

Peter Maxwell Slattery is an international bestselling author who is known as an ET contact experiencer. His ET experiences started at an early age and continue to this day, with hundreds of witnesses to events. He has an overwhelming amount of photographic and video evidence related to UFOs, otherworldly Beings, and apparitions, plus physical trace evidence.

His experiences with extraterrestrials have led him to help people and groups make ET contact themselves, in addition to healing and tapping into their own abilities. Pete has appeared on Channel 7s *Prime News* and *Sunrise*, and many other international television programs. He has made worldwide news, been in numerous documentaries, been written about in magazines, and been a guest on mainstream radio shows, including *Coast-to-Coast*. He is also a musician and, as a filmmaker, he has made a number of documentaries on the subject of E.T.s.

Peter Maxwell Slattery continues to open the world up to the greater reality that "We are not alone" and that "We are all amazing, powerful Beings."

For more information, go to petermaxwellslattery.com

Follow Pete on Facebook, YouTube, Instagram, and Twitter

Printed in Dunstable, United Kingdom